D0888426

You make
the choices that
pick the plot!

Books by the Same Author!

You Are a Cat
in the Zombie Apocalypse!

WRITTEN & ILLUSTRATED BY SHERWIN TJIA

© Sherwin Tjia, 2013
Designed by Sherwin Tjia
First Edition

Library and Archives Canada Cataloguing in Publication

Tjia, Sherwin, author
    You are a cat in the zombie apocalypse! / Sherwin Tjia.

(Pick-a-plot adventures : 2)
ISBN 978-1-894994-77-4 (pbk.)

    1. Graphic novels. I. Title.

PN6733.T55Y69 2013   741.5'971   C2013-906295-5

Printed and bound in Canada by Gauvin Press

Conundrum Press
Greenwich, Nova Scotia
www.conundrumpress.com

Conundrum Press and the author acknowledge the financial
assistance of the Canada Council for the Arts, and the Government
of Canada through the Canada Book Fund toward this publication.

.

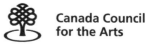

For
Louis Rastelli.
Friend of Cats

WARNING!

Do not read this book beginning to end like a normal novel. This is not an ordinary book, but rather an extraordinary one! You make the choices! You pick the plot!

As you move through this book you will occasionally be asked to make choices. Once you've made your choice, follow the instructions and turn to the page indicated. Your choices will shape, influence and direct what happens to you!

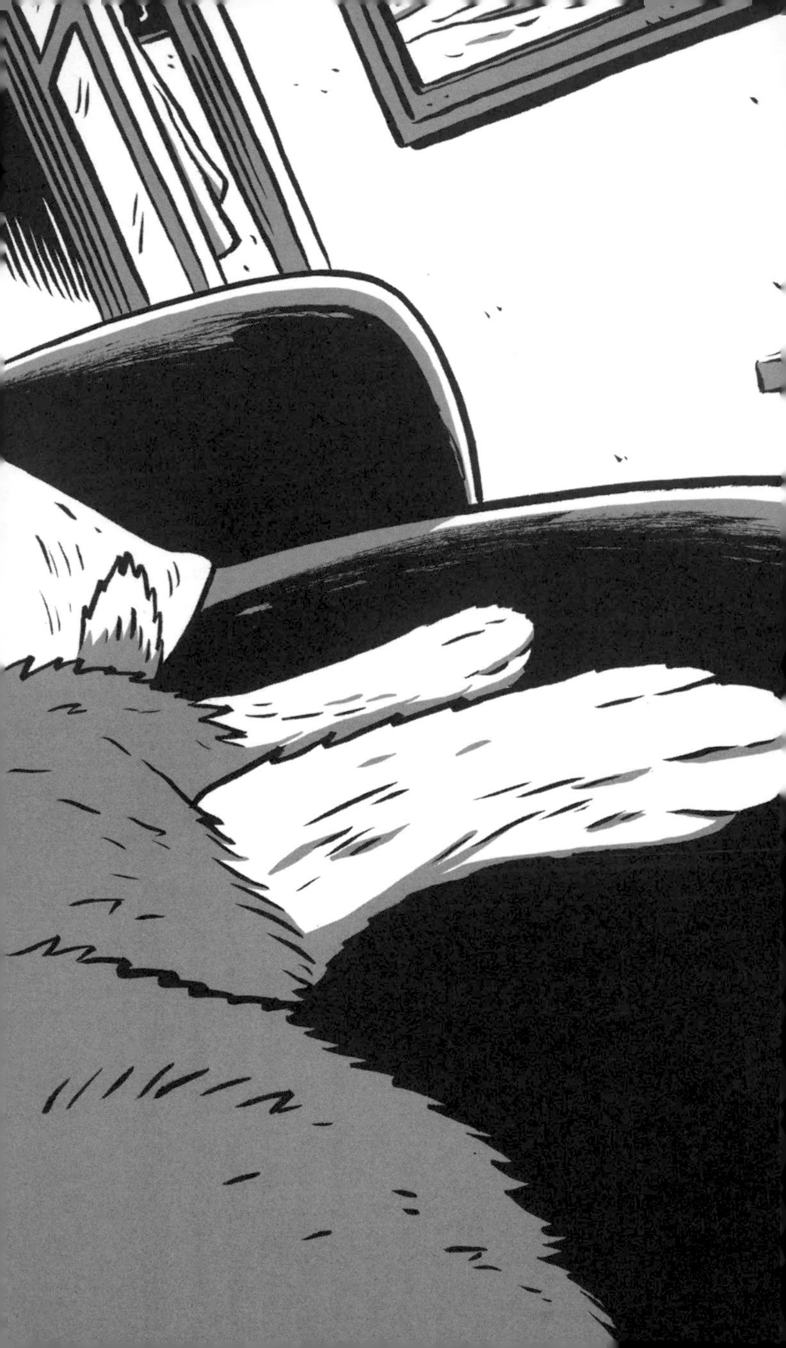

A noise.

You sit, still as a stone in the corner of the couch. Something woke you, and your ears twitch, searching for the source.

For a brief moment you consider getting up and investigating, but then you think better of the idea and close your eyes again.

The muffled thud of a car door closing.

Girls' voices.

This time you get up.

The voices are very close.

One of them is very familiar.

Is it the girl?

You haven't seen the girl in a long time. One day, months ago, she spent a week systematically going through her room, putting some things in boxes, other things in her suitcase, still other things in the trash. The man and woman then helped the girl fill the car with her things.

You didn't like that.

You didn't like it at all.

You hate it when things change.

The boy had done the same thing some time earlier.

His room was still there, but now an abandoned shell of what it used to be. Now you only see him once in a while. He comes home with his big bag, reoccupies his room, raids the fridge, chases you around. This usually lasts a few days — then he puts all the things that smell like him back in his bag and is gone again.

You miss him.

You miss the girl too.

The front door latch unlocks and you stare expectantly.

"...know if anyone will be home — " a voice says.

It's the girl! You get up and drop down to the floor.

In the foyer, the girl comes in, keys jingling from her hand, other hand pulling on her bag. Behind her is a stranger.

"My mom and dad are both at work, so..." the girl trails off when she sees you.

"Holden!" she grins and comes over to you. Grabbing you by the armpits she lifts you up in the air and swings you around, smiling the whole time. Finally the girl brings you to her chest.

As you inhale her scent, you find yourself purring excitedly. Her hair tickles your nose and you look over her shoulder at the stranger.

"Hey kitty," the stranger says.

You take in the strange girl. She has metal piercings in her nose and eyebrow. She levels her gaze at you and, uncomfortable, you look away.

"Holden, meet Amanda," the girl turns you so you're closer to the stranger, who raises her hand to you, scritches you a few times behind the ears.

"This is your cat? How old is he?" the stranger asks.

"I think he's like, six, now."

Restless, you start squirming and the girl drops you to the ground. You walk over to her bag and start smelling it.

"Well," the stranger says. "I should really be hitting the road."

The girl goes over to the stranger and embraces her.

"You're not going anywhere," she says, defiantly.

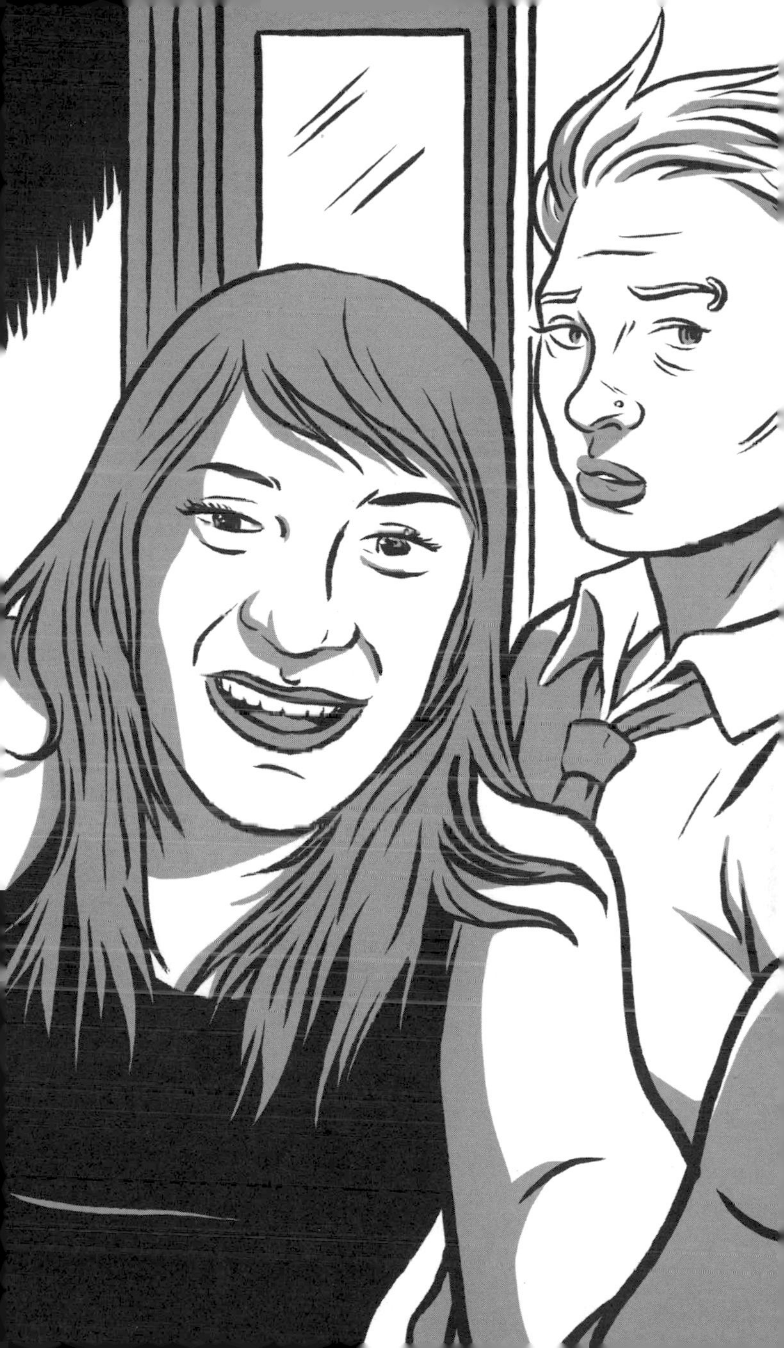

4

"Oh yeah?" the stranger hooks her thumbs in the girl's pants.

"Yeah," the girl kisses the stranger. You walk over to their entwined legs and rub yourself against them.

When they stop kissing, the girl asks the stranger, "So, are you my girlfriend now?"

The stranger laughs uneasily.

"I suppose."

"You don't sound like, excited."

"I've just...never been in a relationship long enough to *call* someone a girlfriend."

Outside, you hear a car pull into the driveway.

The girls hear it too, abruptly separating. The girl moves over to the door, opening it, and the man fills the frame, stumbling in.

"Oh! Dad!" the girl and the stranger take a step back.

"Jules, hon," the man stares at the girl, eyes glazed. "What are you doing here?"

"It's Thanksgiving weekend, Dad. You know that..." The girl trails off as the man leans against the wall. He drops his briefcase with a clatter. "Dad, are you okay?"

The man slides to the floor and sighs heavily.

"Hah, hah," he pants like a dog, mouth open, sweat streaking down his forehead.

"There was," he begins, "an incident...at the office." The man struggles to get the words out. "I'm not...I'm not feeling...." Closing his eyes, the man slumps over and is still.

"Dad!" the girl goes over to the man and puts him gently on his back. "Call 911!" she tells the stranger. The girl puts her ear close to the man's mouth and her forehead creases. "He's not breathing!"

"911's busy," the stranger reports.

"What?!" the girl is pushing down on the man's chest in steady repetitions. "That's impossible."

"All I get is a busy signal," the stranger holds out her cellphone.

Suddenly, a noise comes out of the man. A kind of throaty cough. The girl stops her chest compressions. A flash of hope across her face.

"Dad?!"

Eyes half-lidded, the man uncrumples himself and begins to stand.

"Dad, you really should try to — "

His legs shaky, the man leans against the wall. Eyes half-closed, he takes a look around the room, as if seeing it for the first time. He raises his hands and reaches toward the girl.

"Dad?" the girl says, voice small.

His fingers paw at her breasts and the girl backs off.

"Dad! What are you..."

The stranger knocks him to the ground!

"Amanda, what the hell are you doing?!"

The man is stunned for a second, but then gets up again.

"Yo, Julie — something is really wrong with your dad!"

"I gotta call my mom!"

The girls move around the dining table and the man follows them, like a cat moving to cut off a mouse's escape routes, only more slowly. The girls lead the man to one side, then dash out the other, running to the front door.

"Call your mom from the road!" the stranger yells. "We gotta get out of here!"

"Wait — what?" the girl stops. "We can't leave him here alone! He's sick!"

But the stranger is insistent and manages to pull the girl out the front door.

"He's like a... a fucking zombie!"

You follow after them, not sure if you want to stay with the man, who is a little scary today. He smells different than he usually does.

Outside, the day is blindingly bright, but strangely quiet. The man's car is parked haphazardly, half on the front lawn. The stranger opens the door to her own car and barks at the girl, "Get in!"

The girl stands, stock-still, staring open-mouthed past the car.

"Get in!" the stranger repeats, then looks over the girl's shoulder to see what she's gazing at.

Far down the road, an old woman in a blue jogging suit is stumbling around in circles, arms slightly raised.

"I told you!" the stranger says. "Zombies! Now get in!"

If you decide to get in the car with the girls, turn to page 32.

But part of you is unsettled by all these weird happenings and you are concerned about your girlfriend. If you decide to check up on her, turn to page 8.

If, instead, you are overwhelmed by all this and you want to dart back inside the house, turn to page 7.

You trot to your backyard and step back into the house through your cat door with gratitude. You just want things to be the way they were.

But as you make your way into the kitchen, your ears are pointed and tense. Where is the man?

Then you hear him. He is panting in the living room where you left him. Poking your head around the corner you see him, staring at a wall. What is he doing? You go over to his legs and rub against them. He feels all tense and weird but you do this anyway. Because you just want things to be the way they were.

A noise comes from his wet lips, then he reaches for you.

It's not exactly a stroke on your back. More like a pawing. Then he falls on his knees.

He squints at you.

"Huh, huh," he says. "Ho, ho — Holden."

You look up at the mention of your name. Maybe the man is okay?

Then he leans forward and bites you!

The pain is momentarily overwhelming, then dissipates.

You scamper back into the kitchen, kind of in shock.

You make your way out your cat door and into your backyard where you stumble and fall onto the grass. Then, a moment later, you black out.

Turn to page 25.

8

Shaken, you pad down the alley toward your girlfriend's place. Normally, you can find comfort in a whole host of things — a warm lap, a tasty treat, your girlfriend's purr — but right now you're not sure what's going on, and you need something familiar to hold on to.

A series of irregular wooden fences stretches off into the distance, interrupted occasionally by chain-link fences. You scan for anything unusual as you walk but there's nothing.

The memory of what just transpired flashes in your mind. The man falling. The girls panicking, then running. The strange smell of the man's breath, both sickly and sweet, containing rot and reward.

Finally you arrive at your girlfriend's fence and duck underneath it.

Her yard is fringed on both sides by large fragrant bushes leading to a little patio area where two chairs stand by a single glass table. You cross the large field of grass and pad cautiously up to the closed screen door.

Standing on your hind legs, and climbing up with your claws, you peer inside.

The kitchen sits empty. This is not unusual. But today there is a new smell. The barest hint of sickly sweet.

Inside, you hear the sound of something falling and hitting the hardwood floor.

Was that your girlfriend?

Is she okay?

Loudly, you meow into the dark house.

From inside, the sound of a chair being scraped across the floor. Then, the gentle plodding sound of footsteps. You stare into the darkness, willing your eyes to adjust. Around a corner, a woman slides into view. It's your girlfriend's owner! She has always been very kind to you, more often than not bringing you tasty wet food when you've visited. She is moving very oddly. Stiffly.

You meow again.

The woman starts, as if given sudden life, and shuffles a little quicker. With bleary eyes she sees you and approaches. Through her open mouth, a steady panting issues forth.

"Heh, heh, heh," she pants. Her arms hang like wet spaghetti, swinging as she moves forward.

You stare at her.

Something's wrong. Is she like the man?

You give a third meow and from behind the woman you see your girlfriend!

The off-white cat peeks around the corner, timid.

Finally the woman reaches the screen door. You unclench your claws and drop down to the patio, backing away. The woman walks into the door and pushes against it

"Heh, heh, heh," she stares at you. Her hands scrape against the screen, fingertips smearing into the tiny open holes.

You hiss at her. Then the stench of the woman hits you. It is the smell of a dead squirrel after a few days in the hot sun. Instinctually, you sneeze. Your whiskers almost curl.

To the right of the door, through the open kitchen window, your girlfriend appears. Her wonderful face squeezing through the gap, barely large enough to fit her body.

The woman senses her! Her head moves slowly, but deliberately.

10

You meow again. The woman turns back to you, staring with dead eyes.

Beside her, your girlfriend squeezes her paws out. Scrabbling, she manages to get out! Hitting the ground, she runs over to you.

You inhale her. Around her is that weird sickly smell, but it only drifts around her like loose smoke clinging to her fur, and it's already being blown away by the wind. Underneath is her true smell, and she smells as good as ever, but you can smell the stress in her blood.

You give her a bevy of licks, grooming her cheeks, neck and head. She bumps her head into yours in response.

From the door another sound.

"Huh, huh, huh," the woman pants. There is an urgency now, but she is unable to open the door. Her hands brush uselessly against it.

Finally, you give in to your instinct to flee. You run over to the fence, but when you get there, you realize your girlfriend hasn't followed you.

You look back. She's still by the patio, looking up at her owner. You move back to her. A high-pitched mewl from her mouth. You tug at her but she is immobile. She keeps staring at her owner.

If you decide that you can't wait, and want to go off by yourself, abandon your girlfriend on page 12.

If you decide to wait with your girlfriend, turn to page 13.

If you decide to force your girlfriend to come with you, turn to page 14.

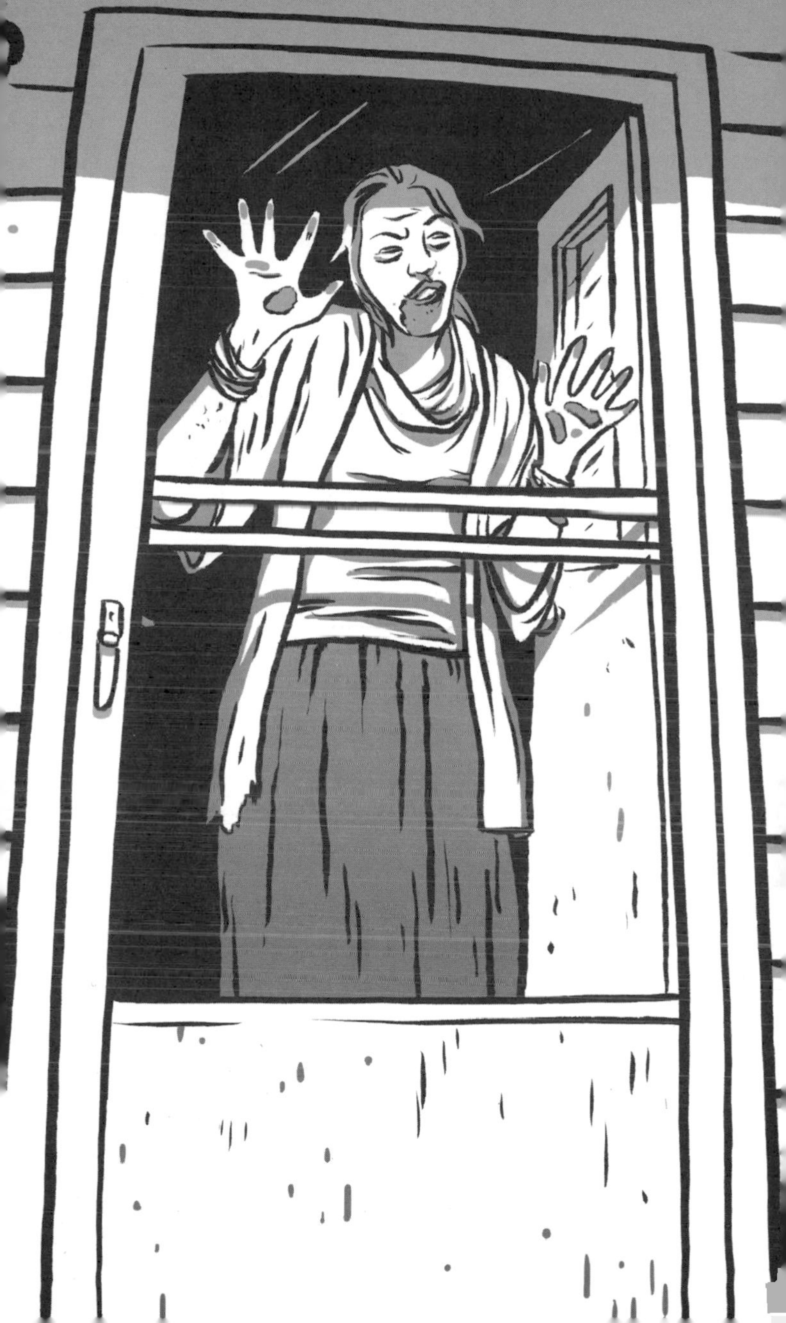

12

With regret, you leave your girlfriend.

She sits, crouched, paws underneath her. Again, her owner's smell wafts out to the both of you. That old familiar smell of the woman who used to bring out plates of wet food for you is all but gone, now replaced by the new, foul one.

You duck underneath the fence and cast a last look at the still, pale cat staring at the screen door.

Bye, girlfriend.

Back in the alley, you consider your options.

You are still longing for something safe, something familiar.

The stress of the last half hour is catching up to you and you are very tired.

You want to find a place to sleep.

But where?

If you decide to take your chances with the man and head back to your own house, turn to page 7.

If instead, you decide to go hang out with a friendly neighbour dude who always gives you treats, head to page 15.

If neither of those options sound good and you'd rather head off down the alley in the hope that things will improve, turn to page 231.

Your girlfriend sits, like she's in a trance, as if she were staring at the two bright lights of a car bearing down on her. You step in front of her, but she keeps staring at the woman.

A tiny, worried whine escapes her.

You settle down beside her.

The woman continues to pant, and paw at the screen door. She trudges forward, but makes no progress. Her hands move like drunken birds, pushing around the door, trying to find a way past, to hopefully trip a latch.

Suddenly, the door opens!

The woman stumbles forward, then finds her footing.

With a leap, your girlfriend jumps backward, then tears through the grass to the fence.

You run after her.

Once in the alley, she gallops away. Fence slats blur by as you struggle to follow her.

Eventually she tires and stops. She is panting.

But it's not a weird panting. It's a normal sort of panting.

You nudge her.

She looks at you, and for the moment, it seems she's herself again.

You lick her whiskers and the two of you settle into a walk down the alley.

Continue down the alley with your girlfriend to page 18.

14

You lean into your girlfriend.

She is still as a rock.

You meow at her, prodding her with your nose.

She refuses to move.

You bat at her with your paw, meowing.

She inches away, but is still fixated on her owner.

Finally, you bite her. You give her shoulder a good chomp.

Meowr!

Your girlfriend snarls at you, then trots away.

You follow her.

She sits in the grass, facing the back fence.

You go over and nudge her.

She hisses.

You lick her ear, and the skin behind it.

She lets you.

You lick some more, around the back and the top of her head.

Your girlfriend moves her head so you can better reach the places she wants licked.

Finally she gets up and moves underneath the fence and into the alley and then keeps going.

You glance quickly back at the house.

The woman is still pawing at the screen door, staring out at you.

You duck under the fence and follow your girlfriend, who has paused a little ways away.

You catch up to her and press your body against hers. Eventually she begins walking and you follow closely behind her.

Walk to the end of the alley on page 18.

A few houses down you enter the yard of a man who has always been kind to you. And not just you — other neighbourhood cats as well. During the winter, he puts out this little cat-sized wood box that's lit with a single light bulb. On the rare occasions you go out while there's still snow on the ground, you can smell the ferals that have taken shelter there.

You pass underneath lawn furniture and jump up onto the windowsill. Inside the kitchen the man is naked and thrusting against a woman who is braced on the kitchen table.

You know this movement. It is familiar to you. You have done it yourself with cats in heat in the past.

They are having sex!

"It's the end of the world," the man says, out of breath.

"Oh god! Oh fuck!" the woman mutters.

"Everything's going to shit."

The woman slams her hand on the table.

Every thrust jars the table a little.

"We could all die tomorrow."

The woman lets out a whine of satisfaction.

"We need to live while we can."

The man has been very kind to you in the past. If you paw on the window to catch his attention, bat at the glass on page 16.

If you decide to keep going down the alley, turn to page 20.

16

You paw at the window.

They don't hear you.

You meow at them.

Louder.

Finally the man looks over. He stops thrusting.

"What are you doing? Why'd you stop?" The woman looks back at him.

"There's a cat — "

"Well get rid of it!" the woman frowns at him, then gives you a dirty look when she spots you. She pushes her bum backwards, as if to get things started again.

The man gives her a few half-hearted thrusts then stops.

"Jesus Christ!" the woman exclaims.

"Hold on! Hold on!" the man comes over to you. "Hey kitty," He puts his hand on the window. You put your paw up on the window too.

"Oh my god, did you see that?" he looks back at the woman, smiling.

She is busy touching herself.

"See what?"

"He put his paw up! He gave me a high five!"

The man's penis swings in front of you. If you were only on the other side of the glass, you would try to catch it like a bird.

"That's great." The woman leans against the kitchen counter. She brings her fingers up to her mouth, licks them, then brings them back between her legs.

The man glances back at her.

"Hey," he says, "Do you think we can — "

"You better not let him in! I'm warning you!"

The man stops mid-sentence, nods, and turns

back to you.

"Hey kitty — I'm sorry. I'm busy. The world is — well, something weird is happening. We're going to try to live our last moments the best way we can. I suggest you do the same."

The man pulls a cord beside the window and white slats come down, blocking your view.

Then, after a moment, his fingers pry open a couple slats and his eyes appear.

"Are you done?" the woman calls over to him.

"Yeah," the man says.

The fingers do a little wave. The man winks, then disappears.

Moments later the grunts resume.

Return to the alley on page 20.

18

When you and your girlfriend emerge from the alley, you hang back a bit, surveying the street.

Nothing is as usual.

One car, crashed into another, is abandoned, with its door open.

A woman stands just inside another alley across the street, phone to her ear.

A distant siren wails.

A man shambles down the street towards you, movements reminiscent of your girlfriend's owner. You keep an eye on him. Right now he seems more interested in the other humans.

A large green truck rumbles along, a man in dappled green talking through a speaker on top.

"Citizens, during this incident, we urge you to stay in your homes. If you need assistance, do not go to area hospitals. We have set up a camp at Kailey Avenue and Bryan. That's Kailey and Bryan. We are going there now. Follow us." The truck roars away.

Skittish, your girlfriend moves quickly underneath a car. You join her in the cool shadow.

If you decide to follow the line of parked cars toward a quieter part of town, stealthily move, car by car to page 65.

Or if you decide to follow the large rumbling green truck, turn to page 21.

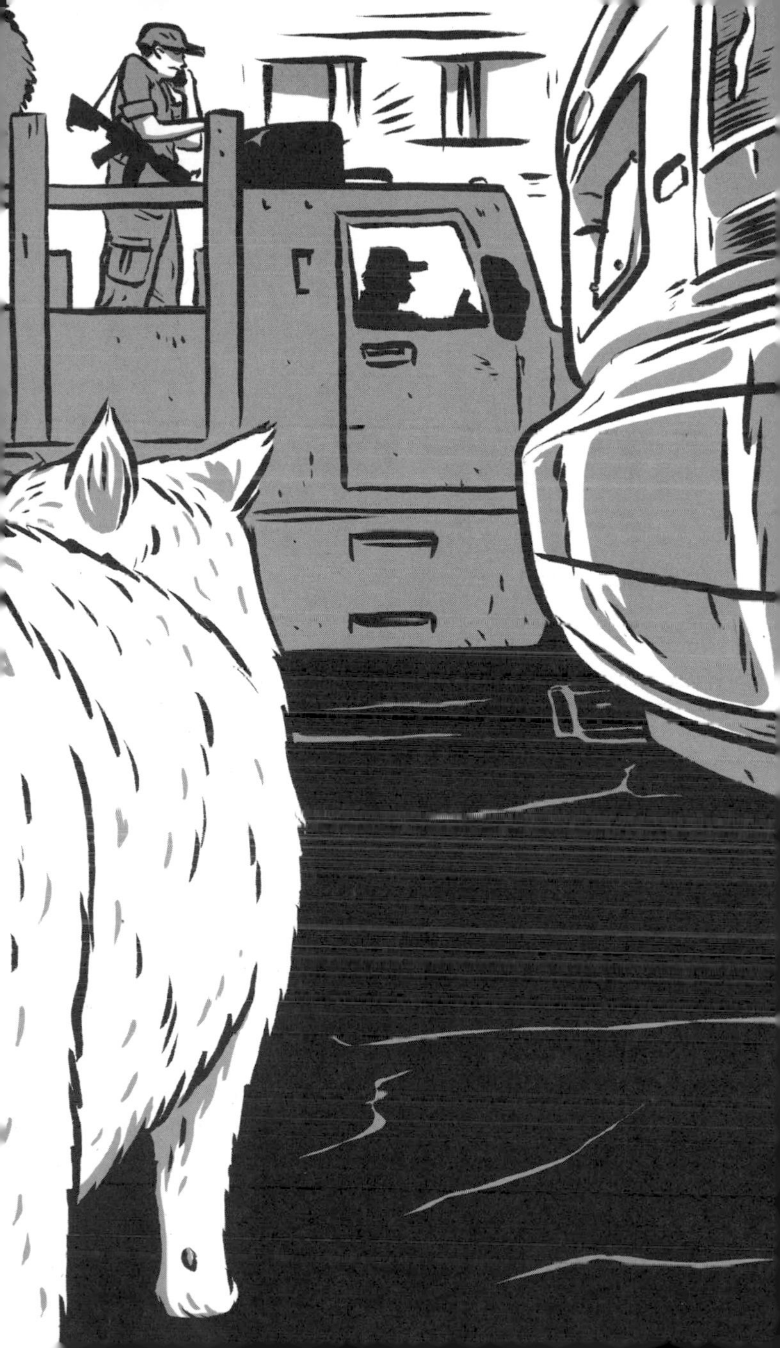

20

As you duck under the fence back to the alley, you glimpse something in your peripheral vision.

It's the tomcat.

You hate him. And fear him.

Regularly, he sprays his scent all over the alley, bombing corners, posts. You don't even know how he manages to get his scent so strong. And distinct. No one smells quite like the tomcat.

You've had some dealings with him in the past. You seldom win. He's bigger and stronger and faster and you always end up running away. You have always been a pathetic beta to his monstrous alpha.

When you see him, you freeze.

Then he sees you.

Something is different though.

Is he one of them? The same scent of rot drifts down toward you.

Your nose twitches. But the tomcat's gait is elegant, smooth.

The dark cat stares at you.

Then, mouth opening like a window, a blood-curdling wail escapes him. It is long and sustained, like the siren of an ambulance. He is making a noise you have never heard a cat make.

And as he screams, he advances!

If you decide to run, go immediately to page 61.

If instead, you want to hide, and hope he ignores you, turn to page 59.

As the large green truck rumbles down the street, you and your girlfriend follow it. While you have always experienced large trucks as terrifying monsters, for some reason, today this particular truck's rumble reminds you of a mother cat's purr.

You and your girlfriend take cover under random cars, creep along piles of garbage and under benches.

You don't want to be noticed. Nothing in the events of recent hours has led you to believe that attracting attention is a smart strategy.

After a long time, following patiently, the truck slows by a familiar park. It's connected to a building that during the day has lots of children running around it. Today, however, the whole area has been transformed.

Even larger green trucks stand at the corners and edges of the perimeter, men perched atop them, and an amazingly long chain-link fence spans the entire territory. Inside, green tents stand in rows.

The green truck you've been following stops at a gate, which opens and lets it in.

A few random infecteds wander out into the open, approaching the gate.

"Zs!" one of the sentries calls out. The men handling the gate quickly close it.

Between you and the camp, a series of dead bodies lie scattered like desolate islands.

"Should I take them out?" another sentry says. He holds a long rifle up to his eye.

"Do it."

A loud crack fills the air and one of the infecteds drops, the top of his head sheared off.

You and your girlfriend move toward the camp, staying close to the bodies, using them as cover. Another crack and another body falls. The two of you press against the shoulder of a corpse, trying to stay out of sight.

"Whoa, did you see the way that one fell? He kind of just crumpled."

"Soldier, stay professional."

"Sorry, sir."

The fence is low to the ground, but you think you can squeeze underneath it. You've crept underneath fences even lower in the past. You're just worried about some of the chain-link barbs. Will it catch on your fur?

But as you crouch to see, suddenly, there's movement. A man emerges from a tent. He spies you.

"Hey, hey!" He turns his weapon in your direction and fires!

A pricking sting on the tip of your ear.

You and your girlfriend run a beeline back to the car as he fires again.

Panting, the two of you lay in the car's shadow, beside a tire.

"Gomez! What was that?"

"Cats, sir. Two cats."

"Fuck."

"We need to lay down some razor-wire or something."

The two of you bide your time and observe the day passing. More infecteds wander out toward the camp, only to be taken down. Then, almost as if they were learning, they start staying away, milling by the buildings on the other side of the street, and not approaching.

Suddenly, you see some feet run toward your hiding spot. They move stealthily, quietly, as if they

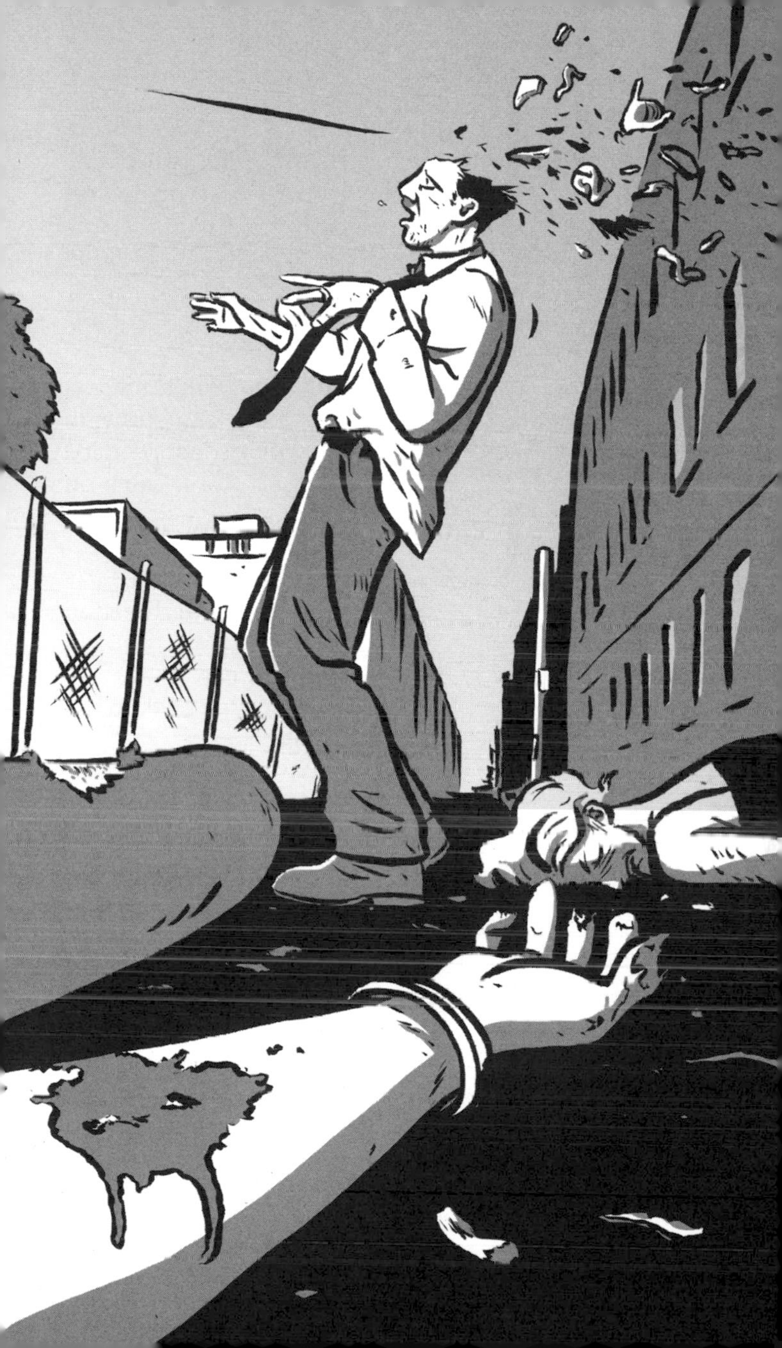

didn't want to be noticed. They are not the shambling feet of an infected.

"Made it," the feet's owner mutters, then opens the door of the car, getting in.

The engine above you roars to life! You begin to dart out from underneath it, but you notice your girlfriend not following. You stop, and go back to her. The car moves away, leaving you exposed.

Your girlfriend has her eyes closed and is breathing with slow, ragged breaths. In the sudden brightness you can see that half of her fur is speckled red with caked blood. She's hurt!

Then, almost as one, the crowd of infecteds by the buildings see you, and begin to approach!

*If you stay with your girlfriend,
stick by her side on page 35.*

*If you decide that she is done for, and that to save
yourself you should run, flee to page 36.*

A blurry splash of colour as you open your eyes.

Unsteadily, you get to your feet. You are unsure what time of day it is, or how long you've been lying in this alley.

As you survey your surroundings, a warmth fills you.

The absolute sense that you are not alone, and that you are loved, grips you.

You sense others. Not far. They're close.

As you take in the fences, it's almost as if you can sense your friends behind them, beyond them, inside houses, on the streets. You sense their presences the way you used to have a scent map of your territory.

The fish store and its pungent, sharp stench.

The bookstore with its musty, dry aroma.

The familiarity of your house. No other house smelled like it.

And now you can feel the others. Some stand in the houses, waiting. Some are in the sky, some are in the sewers. Others are moving, spreading love and connectedness.

So much that's still unfamiliar. Your whole impulse is to turn the unfamiliar into the familiar.

You want everything to smell like you.

And behind it all, underlying everything, a fierce intelligence.

And now you are part of it!

Something journeys through your body and re-knits all your muscles and limbs. In a moment, your senses are even more magnified, connecting you to your larger, but slower collective.

You jog to the end of the alley, your senses reaching out, touching the others, and assessing others still — humans, rats, birds. And those still apart — unconnected. You are trying to fold everyone into one.

By the sidewalk you pause, peering around the brick wall. Cars loom in the street, haphazard. Not the ordered lines you are used to.

Before, when you were a cat, your were very sensitive to noise, but now it's almost as if you can see it, perceive the invisible.

Across the street, in the alley you hear a small whine. The noise streams like a plume from the dumpster.

Quickly, you cross the street and duck into the alley opposite.

You sit in a shadow of a cardboard box and watch the dumpster.

The wail stops, then starts again.

"Shhh, shhh," you hear.

All is quiet for a moment.

Then the squeal of moving metal. A woman pushes open the lid of the dumpster and looks out. She scans the alley. You stay stock still, hoping she won't notice you. She looks delicious.

Finally, she throws one leg out, and clambers to the ground. But she has something in her arms. Something that looks even more delicious.

Wrapped in a blue blanket, the baby sees you immediately and stares.

The woman holds the baby in one arm while trying to retrieve something from inside the dumpster with the other. She can't bend over far enough, however.

"Just for a sec, hon," she kisses the baby and — with infinite care — places it on the ground. Then she boosts herself up onto the dumpster lip and swings back in.

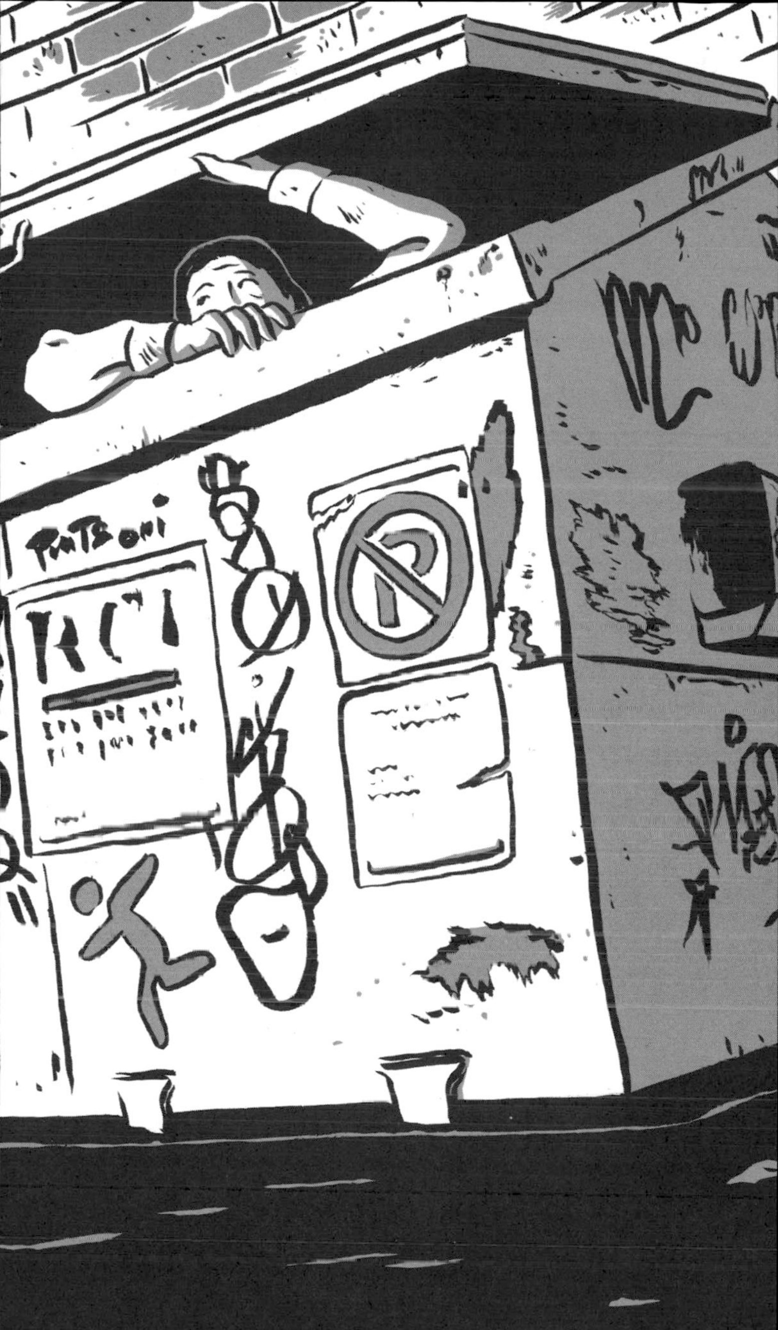

Now!

Now is your chance!

You trot over and look at the kid. He smells so fresh.

He stares up at you with his wide eyes. They are trembling and moist, but you bite the most obvious bit — the kid's nose.

Immediately he starts crying.

The woman's head appears at the top of the dumpster.

"Hey!" she screams. With blazing speed she jumps out and tries to kick you, but you dodge easily and run down the alley. You turn to see her attending to her baby.

"Oh god!" she screams. "No! No!" She brings the baby up to her face and examines his nose. She tries to wipe the blood away. The baby is screaming and screaming.

You love all this noise. It will bring the others. These two need to experience the love you have to share.

In your other life, as a cat, you spent a lot of time alone. You had infinite disdain for dogs, who seemed to need to be around others all the time. But now — that's all changed. You never feel alone and you don't miss it one bit. The others are always with you. And they are closing in.

In fact — you turn, and you see one of your friends just come into the alley from the other end. He pants a greeting at you and moves forward. The woman sees him though, and escapes to the street.

"We gotta go, baby, we gotta — "

She stops at cars and tries their doors one by one. You watch her closely.

Without knowing how, you know that given enough time, she'll manage to escape.

You start wailing. A high howl, designed to travel as far as sound can, to better help the others get here in time.

The woman is startled by the sound. Her movements grow frantic. She runs from car to car. Nothing opens for her.

From other alleys, more figures. All friends.

The woman spins, seeing them.

"No, no."

Finally, a door opens!

She slips into the car and bends down, tries to hide her presence from your friends, but it's too late.

You keep howling and jump up on the car's hood.

She stares at you, wide-eyed.

She screams something at you but you can't hear her over your howl.

You friends come to your location and start pawing at the car windows.

You stop howling and simply gaze at her. She's not looking at you anymore. She is looking at her baby. The baby was crying, but now it's quietened.

Oh.

You can *sense* it.

It's faint, but the baby is becoming a friend.

The woman is weeping and her tears are sliding down her face.

More figures surround the car. They push at it, trying to open it.

Now you can fully feel the baby. It turns its head to look at you, then it looks up at the woman. He starts pawing at her. With his moist, panting mouth he tries to bite at her. She pulls back.

30

He keeps trying, raising his little head to bite at her.

She closes her eyes.

"Oh baby," she mouths. "Oh my baby."

Around you, your friends are pushing the car back and forth. They sync their movements. Inside, the woman and baby sway. The woman's face crumples and she sobs.

You stand on the rocking hood, watching the woman and child.

Then the woman pulls up her shirt, exposing her breast.

Shutting her eyes, she brings the baby to it.

Her face grimaces in pain as the baby bites it. Blood spills and stains her hands and the baby's mouth.

Won't be long now.

Suddenly, a huge boom!

Beside you, a head explodes!

More heads pop, and their bodies fall.

Your friends stop rocking the car.

You turn to see a large green truck. A man on top stands with a long rifle.

If you think it's best to play dead, turn to page 51.

If instead you want to hide, run away to page 173.

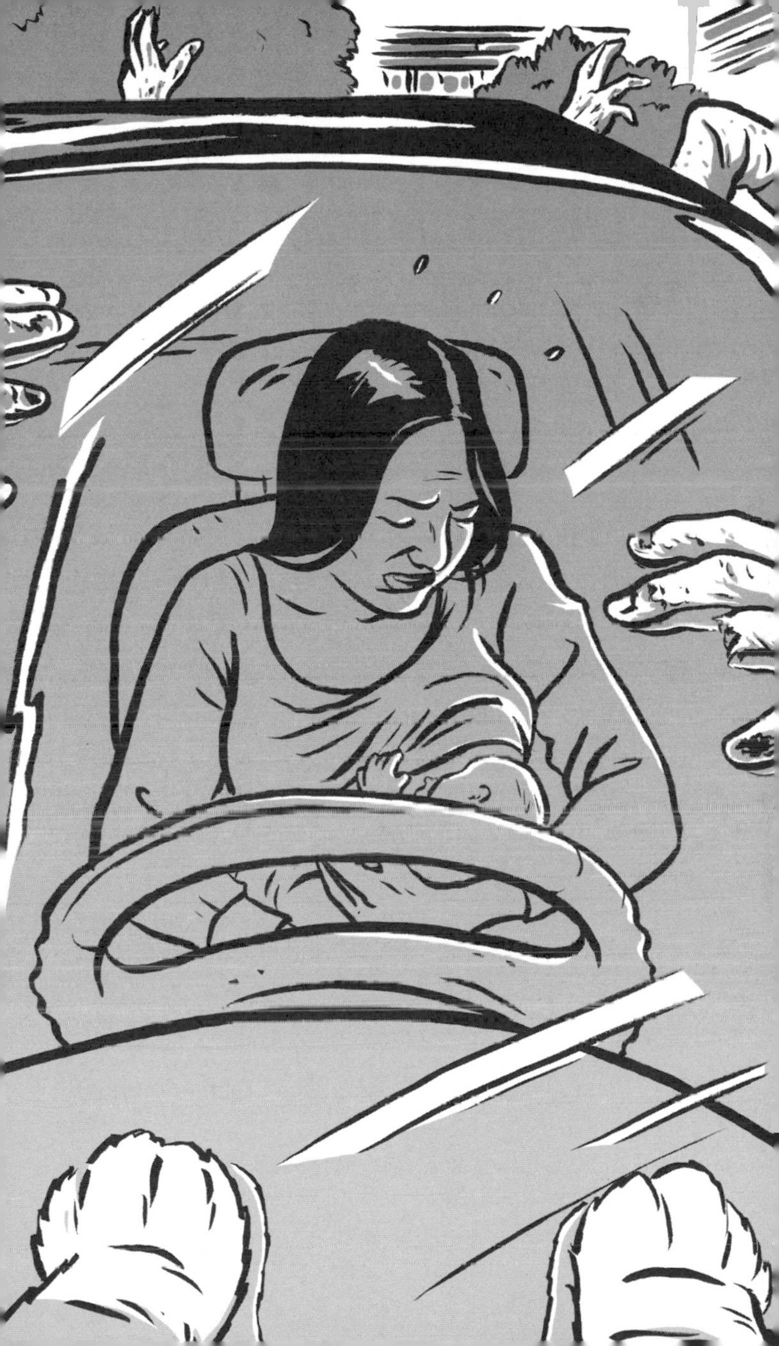

Quickly, you pounce into the car and jump into the backseat.

"Zombies?!" the girl sputters, as she gets in. "That's crazy! That's just insane!"

The stranger sidles in and slams her door closed. All this excitement is too much for you and you jump down onto the rough carpeted floor.

The car jerks into reverse as the stranger pulls it out of the driveway and down the road. She floors it and you flatten your ears at the sudden acceleration.

"Who're you calling?" the stranger asks.

"My mom!"

A pause.

"Is there any answer?"

"Hi — Mom? No — there's something wrong with Dad. No, I'm home...we just arrived. He like, collapsed."

The car suddenly slows, then speeds up again. You sink your claws into the carpet and close your eyes. The sudden movement, out of your control, makes you a little nauseous.

"We tried that, but 911 was busy. You gotta come home! I don't know what to do!"

"Don't tell her to go home!" the stranger says. "Your dad's dangerous!"

"Don't talk about my dad that way!" the girl snaps.

"I'm just trying to help!"

"Mom? Are you there? What's going on?" More silence. "What? Don't go out there Mom! Lock the door! Mom? Fuck! Fuck!"

"What happened?" the stranger asks.

"This — this car just crashed into her firm's building. These guys stumbled out of it. She went to try to help them."

The girl keeps pushing buttons on her phone, keeps bringing it up to her ear, but finally puts it down.

The stranger expertly weaves the car in and out of traffic.

"Where are we going?" the girl asks the stranger.

"My parents' cottage."

The calm voices encourage you to jump up onto the backseat. You bring your face up to the window and stare at the blurry fast-moving world outside.

"Your parents' cottage?" the girl turns to the stranger, a blank look on her face. "Why?"

"Years ago, my parents told me that if anything happened — any kind of shit going down. If like — the end of civilization occurred, that we were supposed to rendezvous at the cottage and wait for them."

"Are you sure we should leave the city?"

"I don't know what else to do."

The girl nods.

"I guess that makes as much sense as anything... Wait, what's going on up there?"

The car slows.

"Some kinda accident..." the stranger mumbles.

"Should we help?" the girl asks.

"I don't..."

From your vantage point you see a sweaty man in a blue shirt stumble up to the car.

The girl lowers her window down slightly. "Are you okay?" she asks him. The man, out of breath, sticks a few fingers through the window.

"Hey! Back off!" the girl says.

"Hah, hah," the man pants, a stream of drool sneaking down his chin.

34

"Shit!" the girl quickly rolls up the window as the car lurches ahead.

In their panic, the girls don't notice the two de-tatched fingers dropping down into the car, bouncing onto the backseat floor.

But you do.

If you are curious and want to examine the man's chopped-off fingers, turn to page 39.

If, however, you decide it's a better idea to ignore them completely, turn to page 47.

You crouch beside your girlfriend. You lick her cheek, trying to rouse her into action but she doesn't seem to notice you, so lost is she in her own pain.

The infected, emboldened by her paralysis, trudge forward.

You nudge her, push her, but she is not moving.

As if anticipating their meal, the first of the infected falls onto his knees! He crawls, like a dog, toward you!

You need to get her away! You bite into the scruff of her neck and yank. Your girlfriend's only response is a fevered roll of the head.

They're getting closer!

You yank — scruff in mouth — your girlfriend away, but she is immobile. In your peripheral vision you see movement. Their slavering panting surrounds you. Finally you unclench your jaws and let go.

You have to run!

But as you tense your muscles to spring away, the surprisingly strong fingers of an infected grabs you around the waist and brings your belly up to its mouth.

As the pain and pleasure of the bite reaches your consciousness, you watch the others dive on your girlfriend.

You pass out from shock.

Turn to page 25.

36

You have to run. It's hopeless.

As you spring away, you see the infected fall upon your girlfriend like a wave. You just hope that it's painless.

More come after you.

Sprinting away, you push down an alley, and see an open door. It leads into a small room with stairs going up. You don't waste a second. You want to get as far away as fast as possible. You zip up those stairs.

Three flights later, you're slowing. At the top, you see a door, propped open by a body. Fresh outside air flows in over it, and you see a roof. You pause, examining the foot. A brown leather shoe leads to a hairy ankle and green pants. It's still. Very still. Nothing moves.

Tentatively, you step over the leg, then, quickly outside.

Looking around, you see the rooftop is empty.

You have a moment to rest.

You examine the man propping open the door. He lies facedown on the tar roofing. Is he dead?

You've seen so much death in the past little while. Everything you've known is over. The memory of your girlfriend being taken by the infected plays over and over in your head.

You move over to the edge of the roof, climbing up onto its metal lip. You peer over it, and see another man on the ground far below. He lies on his back, looking up at you. His hair is long and blonde and splayed out like the branching leaves on a tree. He doesn't move either.

Suddenly you feel dizzy. Then it passes.

You are so tired. This city doesn't sound like it used to. The familiar drone of traffic, birds cheeping,

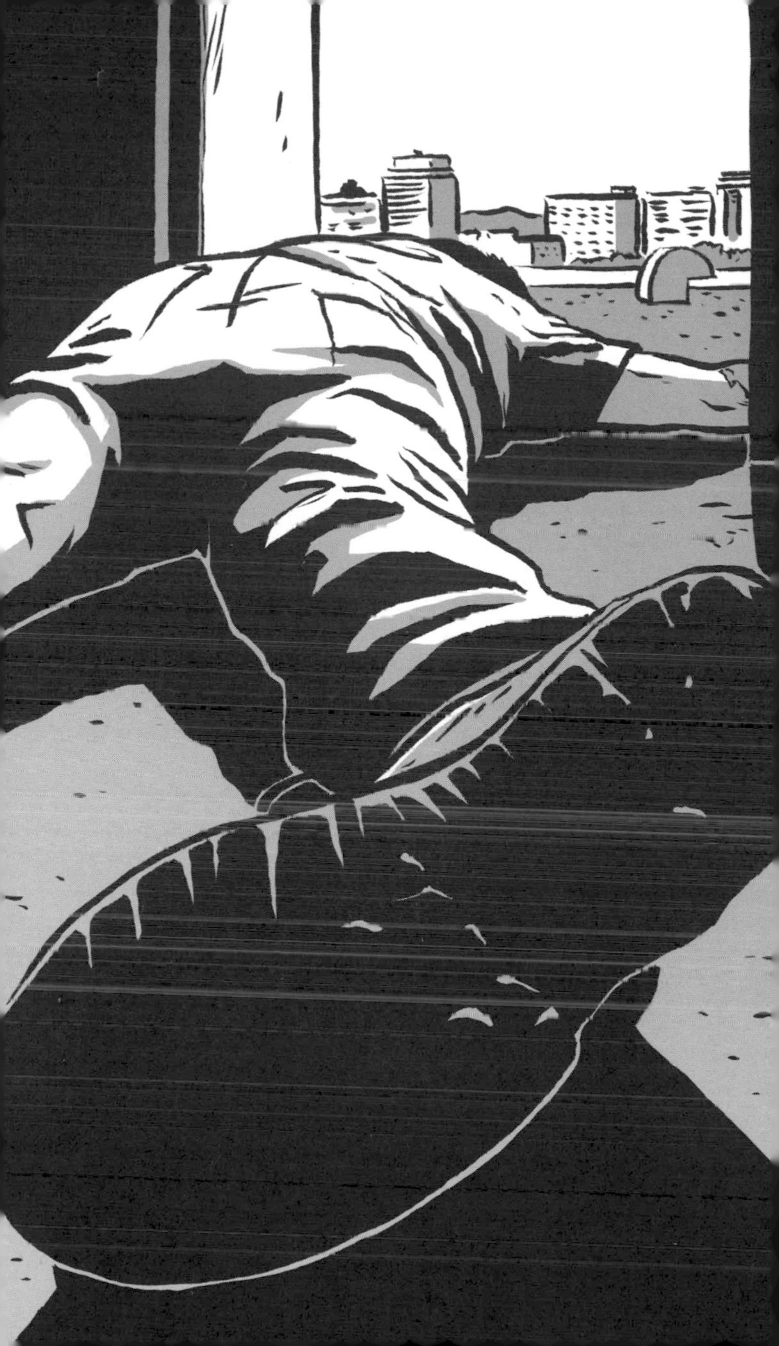

38

random human sounds, are all gone, to be replaced by an eerie silence and the occasional bang or scream.

You hang your paws over the lip.

You could join the man on the street, staring up at you. He looks like he might be at peace. The problems of the world are not his problems.

Your girlfriend is dead. The man is infected, and your family is scattered.

All you want is over.

All you want is over.

If you decide to simply, gently, roll off the roof and let go, turn to page 58.

If instead you decide to head back down the way you came, go to page 90.

The two pale fingers lie inert for a moment, trembling with the movement of the car. You lean close, sniffing, your nose pulsing.

One is almost an entire finger, while the other has only two joints.

They smell very strange. There's blood rimming their serrated edges but also the scent of something else.

"That was crazy!" the girl says. "Everyone's crazy!"

"We're gonna be okay," the stranger states calmly. "We just have to get out of the city. Once we're at the cottage my parents will meet us. They'll know what to do."

Suddenly one of the fingers jerks!

You step back, tripping over your hind legs.

You have seen birds come back to life when you were sure they were dead, but this is too weird. A *detached* wing never moved.

Now the other fingertip moves! Like an inchworm, it begins to crawl toward you.

You back off.

You're apprehensive, but at the same time, very curious. Can you kill it? You are fascinated by it the way you are by bugs.

If you decide to play with the fingers, snag one on 48.

If, instead, you decide to ignore the fingertips, join the girls in the front seats on page 47.

40

You jolt awake. You're still woozy, however.

There's something wrong with your neck, but you move it and you feel it snap back into place.

You smell gasoline.

You lick your lips. You taste blood.

What were you just biting on?

Darkness rings your vision.

The two girls are quiet. The stranger has a huge white bag in front of her while the girl has blood on her nose and her head is bent awkwardly. The glass windshield is spiderwebbed.

Somehow you found your way into the front of the car. Slowly you pull yourself up onto the girl's lap.

You're having trouble breathing.

"Hah, hah," you pant.

You look up at the girl's face.

Blood drips from a gash on her forehead. You lick it. You like it. It kind of energizes you. The wooziness continues, but now it's heady. You kind of tremble, like when you're in the middle of a chase.

You look over at the stranger. A large bite mark scars her neck.

Now you remember. You jumped up onto her shoulder and bit her.

The taste was so good. And then the shouting and then the sudden crash and then the sudden quiet.

You push against the windshield, trying to get outside. It gives way a little.

You lose consciousness, but are dimly aware of time passing, your body moving into the fresh air.

Turn to page 25.

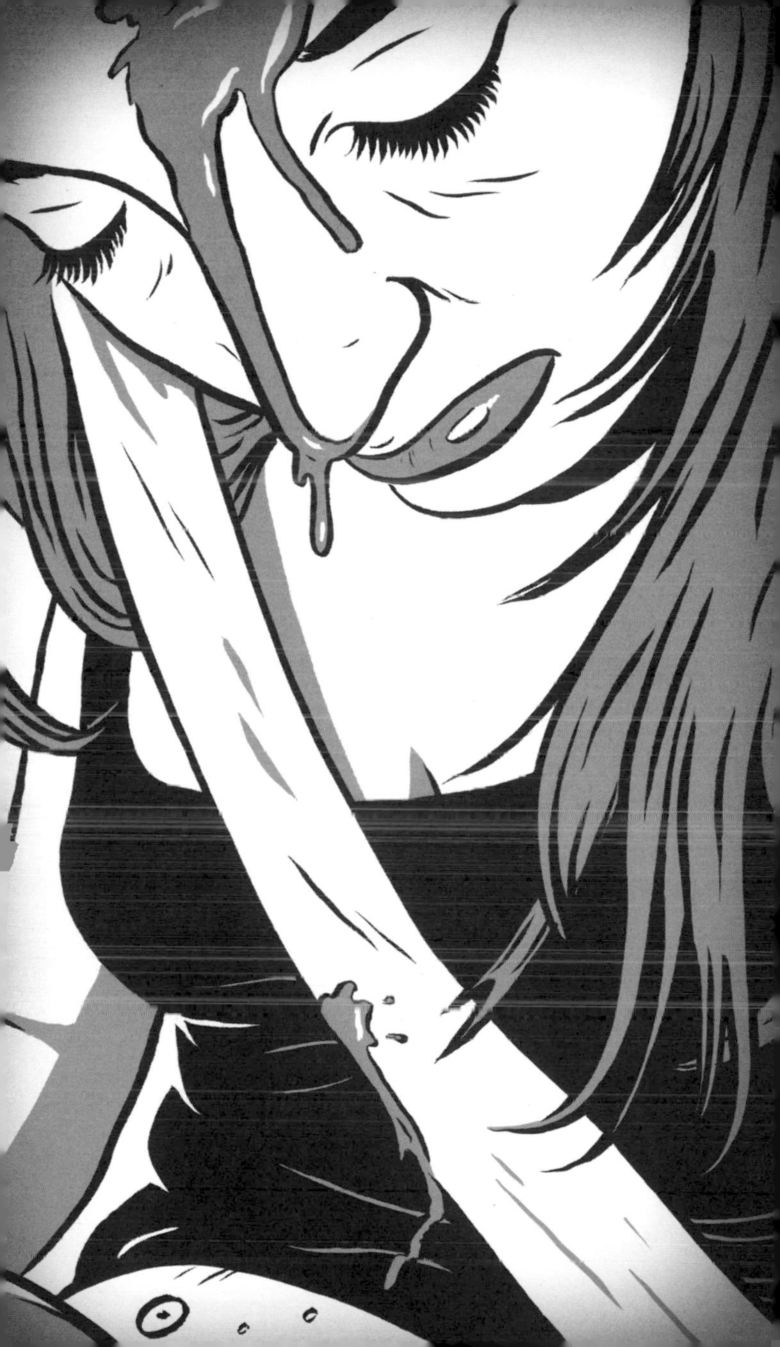

42

The stranger gets up as soon as it's light outside.

You watch her leave the room and you jump down onto the bed, then onto the floor.

Is she going to feed you? You are very hungry.

You stand in the kitchen as the stranger goes through the cupboards. You meow at her.

"Oh shit," the stranger looks at you. "You're hungry. Dunno if we've got anything though."

The stranger looks through the cupboards lower to the floor. "Nope. Definitely got mice though," she says, surveying little black turds. "Sorry kitten. Cupboard's bare."

The stranger gets up and goes to a radio on the counter. She turns it on and static emerges. She turns dials and it's all static. You stare up at her.

Is she going to feed you? How long do you have to wait?

Then the stranger puts on her shoes.

Is she not going to feed you?

The stranger goes to the door. She's going outside.

She's not going to feed you.

You are very hungry. If you want to wake up the girl, in the hopes that she'll feed you, turn to page 45.

If, instead, you feel you might have a better chance of finding food if you go outside and explore, go out with the stranger to page 88.

You wander deeper into the woods. The trees are thin here, and you sometimes look back, noting where the cabin is. You can follow your own scent back, but that might get compromised. You consider taking a piss on a nearby tree, so you have a marker, but because you've gone so long without water, you don't have much in your bladder to spare.

Finally you break through a last stand of trees and face a river.

This is very exciting! You have never seen a river before.

True, on rainy days in the summer you have witnessed torrents of water flowing down streets and into sewers. You have witnessed the water in the tub filled almost to overflowing. You have seen the cascade of water coming from high above in the shower. But you have never witnessed so much water moving so fast, over rocks, and travelling off to a point behind a bend, sunlight reflecting off of it, dazzling you. This place is amazing.

You wander over to it. The ground is damp under your footpads, sand sticking to you as you venture close.

The moving water is hypnotic, and slightly scary. But closer to you, the water moves a little slower, and you lick at it.

It is cool and delicious. You are so thirsty. You lap up more of it.

You do this for a long time.

When you've had your fill you walk alongside the river a bit.

And then you spy a small silver fish writhing among the rocks up ahead.

Immediately your stomach growls.

44

You walk over to it and, waiting for your moment, put your paw on it!

It stares back at you with its dead eyes, its mouth opening, closing. It trembles.

It smells kind of funny though. Back home, you've spent a lot of time by the back door of the fish store, so you are familiar with all the varying smells of fish decay, and this fish smells nothing like it.

Then you hear voices. Male voices. Up ahead and around the bend in the river.

Do you want to eat the fish?
Chomp down on page 122.

If you ignore the fish for now, and instead go visit the voices, turn to page 127.

You sniff around the kitchen. Maybe the stranger missed something?

Leaping on top of the counter, you examine the dry sink. You smell ancient remnants of food. A hint of fish. Watermelon. Something else. But that's it.

Through the kitchen window you see the stranger bend down and disappear underneath the porch. Where did she go? It looks like she crawled underneath the cabin. Is she going to come back?

A few moments later she reappears with a long black case.

The stranger comes back inside and puts the case on the kitchen counter. With one hand she wipes off stray cobwebs and caked-on dust. Then she turns on the tap and washes her hands.

You go over to the sink and lap up the water. You're so thirsty. It's not great, but you'll take it.

The stranger opens the case and pulls a long metal tube out of it, attaching it to a wooden piece. You pause in your drinking to sniff at it. It reeks of a pungent oil.

The stranger places the wood end against her shoulder and lifts the other end to you. The tube isn't just one tube, it is actually two tubes. The holes stare at you like dark eyes, inches from your face. You sniff the metal.

"Boom!" the stranger whispers.

She lifts the tube a bit, then lets it fall.

"Hey!"

The girl comes striding out of the bedroom.

"Hey, you're up," the stranger says.

"Don't do that with my cat!"

"Babe, it's not loaded," The stranger cracks the shotgun open into a V and shows it to the girl.

"I don't care. Don't pretend to kill my cat."

"Awright. Awright."

You examine the case, stepping gingerly into it. The inside is covered with a soft brown fur. There are a few open spaces recessed inside, but they are too narrow for your body. You try to settle in them anyway. It's uncomfortable, so you get up.

"Where'd you get that, anyway?"

"Hiding spot," the stranger says. She retrieves a small paper box inside the case and pulls out little red tubes, filling her pockets with them.

"Don't like, load it," the girl says.

"It's useless if it's not loaded."

A rhythmic beat fills the air, catching the stranger's attention. She tosses the shotgun on the couch and reaches into her pocket for her phone.

"Dad?! Dad!"

A warbly static.

"Dad!"

The stranger pulls the phone from her ear and looks at it. She puts it up to her ear again. "Dad?"

"What happened?" the girl asks.

"I just heard him say like — 'honey.'"

"That's all he said?"

"Yah." The stranger presses more buttons. "I'm gonna try to call him back."

You grow bored of all this.

---

*If you decide to explore the rest of the cabin,
turn to page 194.*

*If you decide to stay with the girls in the main
room, settle in on page 204.*

You jump up into the space between the two girls.

Outside, there are more cars on the street. But not all of them are moving. Some are parked awkwardly. Others are keeping pace with the car you're in.

Your thoughts drift to your girlfriend. With everything changing so quickly, you wonder if she's been affected by all this. You have a deep longing to be next to her.

The stranger glances idly at you as she manages the sporadic traffic.

"How come your cat doesn't have a collar? Don't they usually have them?"

"Oh," the girl says. Her voice is strained and a small crease hovers on her brow. "My mom told me that it broke the other day and I guess they haven't gone to get another one yet."

Suddenly the car directly in front comes to a stop.

"Shit!" the stranger yells, and slams the brakes. You sink your claws into the padded armrest you're perched on. "Fuck!" she says, exasperated. She honks the horn. All this noise freaks you out and you jump into the back again.

Then the back door opens.

"Please!" a woman says, half stepping into the car, "Can you give me a ride? I need a ride."

In your life, anytime a door opens, you are half-drawn to it.

It's not to late to go see her — if you want to go check on your girlfriend, make your escape now to page 52!

But if you'd rather stay in the car, hold tight on page 54.

48

Experimentally, you dig a claw into the smaller of the two fingers. It wiggles like a worm.

How is it even moving?

You aren't scared anymore.

You paw at it, rolling it.

The larger finger suddenly moves, as if both fingers were part of the same hand.

You bat at it, too.

Soon you are on your haunches, watching the fingers with fascination.

You put a paw on them, taking grim satisfaction in feeling them struggle under your pads.

"I have to call my brother," the girl says.

"Where's he?"

"Guelph. He was supposed to come home this weekend too. I think he's bussing it, though. I'm not sure when his bus was supposed to leave."

You are really enjoying this now. You move the fingers around a bit more and then bring one to your mouth, biting it, holding it in with your paws!

It wiggles.

Your rough tongue holds it in place, and you bite even deeper. Its grim ichor fills your mouth, glazing your tongue.

You start to feel woozy.

You are in trouble. You jump into the front seat. Can the girl help you?

You need help. You're blacking out.

Turn to page 40.

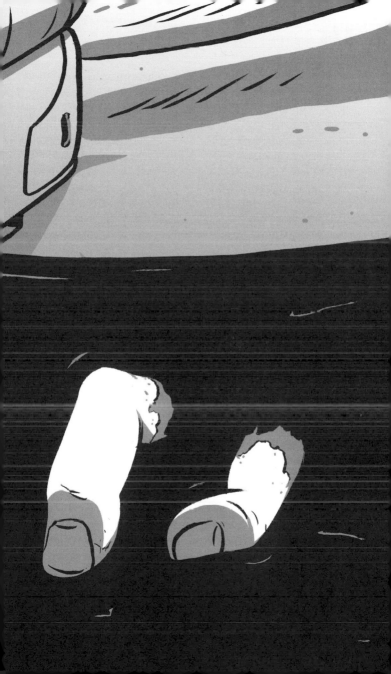

50

You race to open roof, all the while being followed by the infected.

The woman jumps on board the helicopter and it starts to lift off! A few infected grab onto the landing strut, however. Their added weight makes it hard for the chopper to lift off cleanly. A man inside pulls out a small axe and chops at the infecteds' arms!

Suddenly — a familiar smell. You turn around.

It's your girlfriend! But it's *not* your girlfriend.

She's one of them now.

The helicopter swings away from the building, dropping infected. Then it swings back toward you!

You have a chance!

Turning, you leap onto the landing strut! But it's so slippery! You try to hold onto it like a tree branch, but it's almost impossible.

The helicopter begins to lift off, taking you away from your girlfriend and the horde.

Suddenly the man in blue appears in the doorway again.

"Fuck!" he exclaims when he sees you. "They're like barnacles!" Swinging the axe, he embeds it deep in your back. You lose all muscle power.

You let go of the strut.

Wheeling, you fall toward your girlfriend and the roof and the horde.

Time slows. Flashes from your life drift across your consciousness. As the group underneath you gets larger at an alarming rate, you are calm.

A lap. A kill. A nap. A chase.

It was a good life.

You are sorry that this is —

THE END

You drop down onto the car hood.

Little specks of blood mist over you as your friends' heads are blown off.

A little pain in your heart each time, like candles going out.

Finally they are all down. Bodies sprawl atop each other, strewn around the car.

"Whoo! Nice shooting!" someone in the truck says.

"One shot, one kill, motherfucka!" the man holding the rifle says.

"More like, fifteen kills," the other person laughs.

The man with the rifle gets out of the truck and slings his long gun across his back. He reaches for his thigh holster and pulls out a smaller gun.

He jogs over to the car and peers inside.

"Ma'am!"

The woman looks at him with glazed eyes. He takes in her bloody nipple, the panting baby.

"Oh god," he mutters and shakes his head.

"What is it?" a voice crackles in his radio.

"Something terrible," the man responds.

One of your friends on the ground grabs at his ankle!

The man jumps back.

"Fuck! Some of them aren't dead!"

With his small gun, he systematically shoots your friends' heads again. Making sure.

Then, he aims through the windshield, killing the mother and baby.

And then, almost as an afterthought, he kills you, too.

THE END

Seizing your chance, you pounce through the open car door.

"Whoa!" The woman backs off.

As you find cover under a parked car, you see the girls speed off.

"Fucking bitches!" The woman screams after them. "Fucking — " She breaks off and begins sobbing.

You pause for a second, taking things in.

A litany of honks as the woman wanders into the road, trying to flag another car down, unsuccessfully trying to open doors.

Slowly you become aware of a man coming out of an alley, moving slowly toward the woman. His gait is odd. A kind of lurching saunter. Nothing sudden. For this reason he gets very close to the woman before she notices him. His hands reach out to her.

"Hey! Hey!" she backs off into traffic. Again the litany of honks.

The man follows her.

Now the woman is running.

The man follows, but is bumped by a car.

He swivels his head and refocusses his attention on those inside the car. Wheels squealing, they drive right into him!

The man rolls onto the hood and bounces off, falling to the side as the car continues on.

He is still for a moment, but then begins the gradual process of finding his feet again.

You figure you've seen enough.

Staying close to any parked cars, you dart from wheel to wheel back in the direction of your home. You hadn't gone far with the girls. The area feels familiar. This is the outer edge of the area you know.

Finally you get to the alley you were looking for. Following this will take you to your girlfriend.

Continue to page 8.

"Hey, get out!" the girl cries from the front seat. But already the woman has opened the door and is putting her foot in.

"Just get me out of this — "

Without a word, the stranger reaches over in front of the girl. She pushes a button and a small cavity opens in the dash. She grabs a container and turns to the woman getting in. A sharp orange spray jets out and hits the woman in the face!

Instinctively you close your eyes and dive to the floor.

The woman screams and jumps out of the car.

The car leaps forward, hitting another car! The stranger turns the wheel and the car bumps up onto the sidewalk, moving some distance, then jolts back down onto the road.

The car is beginning to fill with acrid, cloying fumes. Your eyes and nose are tearing up. With your forepaws, you try to cover your face but it is everywhere. Mucus fills your nose, throat and mouth and you retch. This is a thousand times worse than coughing up a hairball.

"Fuck!" the stranger sputters. "I'll open the windows." Suddenly, all the windows descend.

As fresh air circulates in, slowly you can breathe again.

The girl reaches back and shuts the back door soundly.

"You should probably hold the pepper spray," the stranger hands the girl the container.

"That was pretty fucking cool," the girl replies. "And fucking scary."

"Is your cat still in the car?"

The girl looks back and sees you.

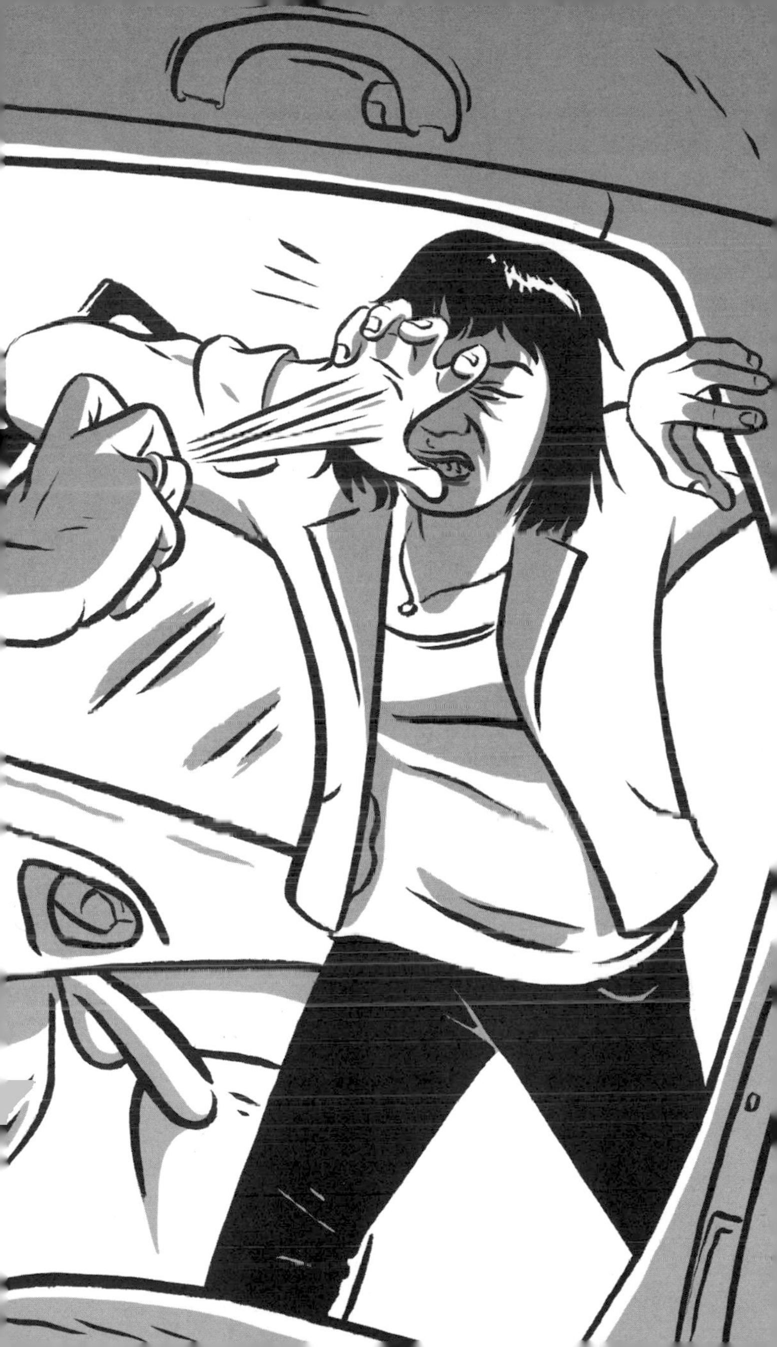

"Ohhh," she laughs. "Poor Holden. The spray bothering you?"

You are still rubbing your eyes and nose, occasionally sneezing.

The girl lowers her chair back and reaches over to rub your head. With her finger, she wipes away some of the snot around your nose.

You rub the side of your head against the hard knuckle of her hand a couple times.

"Okay," the stranger says. "Here's the highway. Looks pretty good."

The car continues, unimpeded now.

You drive for a good long time. Occasionally, cars with flashing lights shoot by in the opposite direction. After a while, you end up in the girl's lap. Now that it's quiet, it seems pretty safe.

"City seems like the wrong place to be right now," the stranger comments.

The girl bites her lips.

"Where are your parents going to be coming from?"

"What day is today? Friday?"

The girl nods.

"Dad's gonna be...he's gonna be playing tennis at the park. My mom's gonna be at work. At the school."

"Oh god," the girl says. "Those kids. How're they going to find their parents?"

"I don't know. I don't know."

By now, the air has cleared and the windows are back up. The low droning of the car has put you to sleep once or twice.

"We're gonna need gas soon," the stranger says. "I don't want to stop at the rest stops. I don't know. They seem a little sketchy to me."

"What do you want to do?"

"Let's try one of these smaller gas stations. Off the beaten track."

The car slows and you open your eyes. You sit up on the girl's lap and look out the window. Going much slower now, the car winds its way down a ramp and along a desolate road. Ahead is a small building with a large canopy. The car pulls up underneath the canopy and stops.

The girls undo their belts and the girl sets you aside.

"We're just going in for a sec, Holden. You stay here."

If you feel like stretching your legs after such a long drive, jump out with the girls on page 64.

If instead, you are still a little apprehensive about this strange new world, stay inside the car on page 67.

58

Every instinct says no, but something else, a giant sadness, nudges you over.

No! Wait!

You don't want to do this. You claw at the ledge, but your centre of gravity has shifted too far. Your hind legs scrabble at the brick wall!

It's too late!

You fall!

Rotating in mid-air, you stretch your tail out to help you balance.

You spread your arms and legs out, trying to glide down.

But before you know it, you've hit the ground.

And then you don't know anything ever again.

THE END

Quickly, you duck back under the fence and dash into a shrub.

It's leafy, green and thick, and you try to make yourself as small as possible inside.

Outside, the wailing halts.

Through the tiniest of gaps, you peer into the yard.

Paranoid, you scan the area at the foot of the fence.

Is he going to follow you?

Possibly he got bored and left.

You settle down on your belly and wait.

You've had to wait for many things over the years. Before your family installed the cat door you used to have to wait to be let in. There have been a lot of chilly days and hungry hours. You've gotten used to waiting. Usually you just look around to see if you can spot birds. You try not to get tricked by the idle movement of leaves, grass, flowers, branches.

And now you wait again.

You think he must be gone.

It's been quite a while.

You poke your head out. Instead of walking across the grass, you sidle up to the fence and walk along it, to lower your profile.

Then, reaching the gap under the fence, you duck your head out, looking both ways.

The alley extends out to the street on either side.

No sign of the tomcat.

Your heart — which had somehow been clenched this whole time — relaxes.

But as you begin to walk out in the open, the loud siren of a wail begins again!

Ears perked, you look up!

60

The tomcat, perched on the fence, leaps down onto you!

You don't have time to move.

His teeth are on you, like a vampire bat.

He gnaws on you, and somehow you can't move at all.

Maybe it's the surprise.

Maybe it's something else.

Body wracked with stress and shock, you pass out.

Turn to page 25.

You turn tail and run. You don't like to mess with the tomcat under *regular* circumstances, and these are definitely odd times.

Behind you, the tom stops wailing and chases you!

Is he one of them? He *smells* like them. He smells like the man. He smells like your girlfriend's owner. He smells *bad*. But each one of them was crippled by a shambling, pained gait. The tomcat is running like he is brand new in the world.

Nothing makes sense.

You are getting tired.

You're a good sprinter, but not used to running for extended periods.

You duck under a fence into a backyard. Maybe you can lose him. But the tom follows with uncanny precision.

Then suddenly, the tom slows and starts wailing again.

Weird.

You keep running, taking this opportunity to get away. But the wail follows you, haunts you.

It reminds you of a dog's fevered howl.

You slip through a hole in a fence and then go back into the alley.

You head back the way you came, but two men stride into view, cutting off your exit. They move slowly, and there is a dog with them.

You freeze.

In the yard, the tomcat has stopped howling.

Is he calling them?

You turn, ready to run the other way, and the tomcat is right there, terrifyingly close.

His eyes are bright red, as if bathed in blood.

Where can you go? Can you slip around him?

In that moment of indecision, the tomcat, moving with blinding speed, leaps on you!

You push his open mouth away with your paws, keep his weight from settling on you with your hind legs. But he is tenacious.

But suddenly his weight is gone.

A flash of off-white fur pushes the dark grey tom off you.

Your girlfriend! She followed you! She saved you!

She knocks the tom to the ground, then in one smooth motion, runs past him.

You flip over and chase her.

When you are safe, you look back.

The two men, the dog, and the tomcat stand in a circle. Almost like they're talking. You should get out of here before they decide to resume a chase.

Your girlfriend nudges you and the two of you advance to the alley mouth.

To your left, the street seems a little more sedate. You might find a safe haven in that direction.

Alternately, on your right, a fire escape ascends the side of a building invitingly.

Do you head to the quieter suburban streets?
Turn to page 65.

If instead, you decide to get a higher vantage point and go up the fire escape, climb it to page 99.

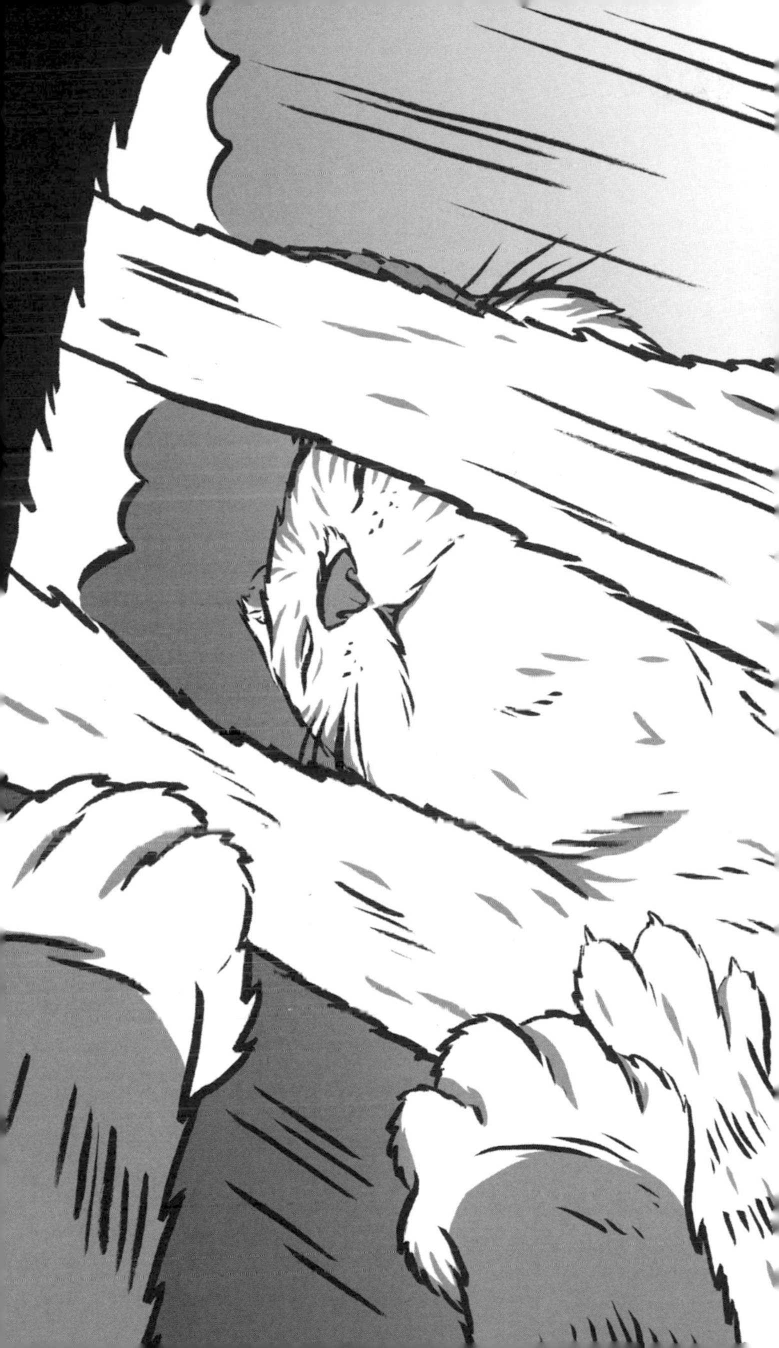

As the girl emerges from the car you slip out between her legs.

"Hey!" she says sharply, "Holden!"

You hear her. You know she's upset, but you keep going. The whole place smells like gasoline, like the underside of parked cars.

"Babe, you better get your cat or it's gonna be hell getting him back in the car."

"I know, I know."

Suddenly the girl's voice changes.

"Holdy," she says, high and kind. Like whenever she gives you a treat. Does she have a treat for you now? "Mr. Catfield. Come here. C'mere please."

You turn. The girl has bent down and has her hand out. Her fingers rub together. Is there a treat there?

You move closer, and sniff at her hands.

Easily, she grabs you under the belly and lifts you up!

She throws you back into the car and the stranger slams the door behind you.

They slap hands and then go toward the building.

You press your nose up against the window, your paws on the armrest. Something under your feet gives way and the glass window shoots down! Startled, you jump back.

Now there is a cat-sized opening in the window.

If you choose to jump out and follow the girls into the building, turn to page 68.

If you'd rather stay in the car, not wanting to risk another humiliation, go to page 67.

There. That's better.

This street is a quiet one. You and your girlfriend have been wandering for the last little while, stopping at every intersection, choosing to go down the quieter street each time. You need some peace.

Actually, what you *need* is a day to do *nothing*, to just sit at home on the couch, to clean yourself, to eat something and to sleep. You just want the regular.

As you've been wandering, it's gotten darker and darker, and cooler and colder. The sun has disappeared, and the orange sky's complexion is rapidly turning blue like a bruise.

In the distance, you hear the low bass of a loud rumble. The occasional sharp crack. But those noises are far enough away to cause you no concern.

Now the two of you stop beside a bush.

Ahead, at the end of this quietest street of quiet streets is a grey minivan with its doors open in someone's driveway. A thick clump of trees hangs overtop, almost hiding it. You see a few humans moving stuff into it, trying their best to be quiet. The dark of the evening aids them in this. Their house isn't even located near a streetlight. You are intrigued by this stealthy family.

As your girlfriend moves forward to get closer, you follow.

"Mom, this?" a girl holds something up.

"No, Katie. We're leaving that behind."

The girl goes back in the house while the woman arranges something in front of the minivan.

You look up through its open back doors at the round shapes of items inside.

"Almost done anyway," the woman mutters to herself. "Should probably go."

66

When the woman goes inside the house, your girlfriend jumps up into the minivan!

If you follow her and jump inside as well, turn to page 102.

If you decide that it's too risky, and you stay out of the vehicle, turn to 109.

You settle down on the seat, still warm from the girl's bum. Faint traces of the pepper spray still linger in the car, mixing with the scent of gasoline.

It is a while before the girls come back, but when they do, they carry large white plastic bags.

"Well that was nice," the girl says as the stranger fiddles with something on the side of the car. "At least not *everyone's* crazy."

The smell of gasoline is suddenly more intense, and you hear a low humming sound.

Moments later, everyone is back in the car and you're moving again.

The girls eat stiff wafers out of crinkly bags. They offer you some but the smell is too sharp and unfamiliar. You are getting thirsty though.

"Can you check the map?" the stranger says to the girl.

"Sure," she replies, opening a book. "What am I looking for?"

"We're on the 7. We're looking for the 7A. And then Simcoe. Look in Lindsay."

The girl nods.

"You've got a while yet."

"Okay."

"When do you think we'll get there?"

"Probably just before the sun sets. In a couple hours."

"Okay."

The rocking of the car lulls you asleep again.

Turn to page 72.

68

Scampering, you rush to keep up with the girls.

The stranger opens the building door and they both step inside. As the door moves to close you dash forward and manage to sidle in before it shuts!

You are feeling rather pleased with yourself when you hear the girl say, "Oh shit!"

You look up.

A blue smoke fills the room. A man stands in front of the counter, a rifle in his hand. He points it at the girls.

"Don't move!" he bellows. The girls raise their hands.

"Look, we just — " the stranger begins.

"Don't look at me!" the man barks. "Look over there!" He gestures to a corner. Both girls comply. The man edges to the door.

You move along the counter, looking for a quiet corner to hide. You're not sure what's going on, but all the raised voices scare you, and the stress bleeds off the girls in waves.

You stop at the edge of the counter. An old man lies there, one arm outstretched. His eyes open — glassy and unmoving.

You wander over to the girls.

"Shit, what — ?" the man moves the rifle to follow you.

"Don't shoot him!" the girl yells. She moves to grab you.

"Julie, no!"

An ear-splitting *bang!*

The girl drops you, and crumples on the ground, holding her chest, which is wetly red.

"You asshole!" the stranger rushes the man, trying to grab the gun.

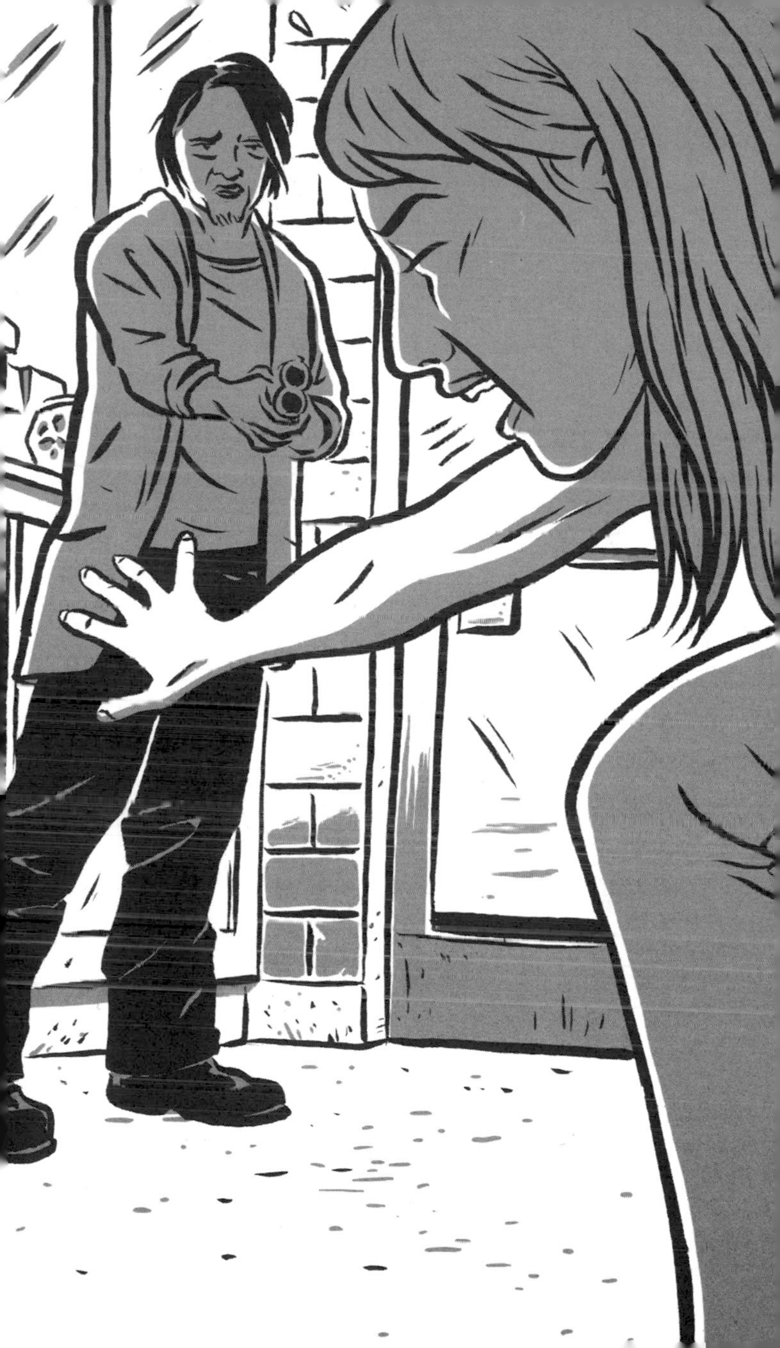

Another bang!

The stranger grabs her neck. A geyser of blood jets from between her fingers. She falls to her knees, and then slumps to her side.

By now you've run to the back of the room. You huddle beside a still-wet mop, smelling mostly of mildew. The room is now even smokier.

"Oh god," the man mutters to himself. "Now I've gone and done it."

The man puts the gun on the counter and leans against it. He doesnt move for a long time. Long enough for the shadows painting the floor to move a few inches.

You want to go over to the girls but you are afraid to move. You are afraid the man will make the gun bark again. You want to hide but there's nowhere to hide.

Finally the man starts moving again. He leaves the gun where it is.

You shrink back behind the mop.

He looks on the shelves and picks something out. That scrape of metal tin on metal rim. You know it very well. When he lifts the metal tab you're sure of it. *Wet food.*

You come out of hiding. The man squats down beside the bodies of the girls and opens the can, leaving it on the floor.

"Hey cat," he says gently. He smiles at you.

The beautiful smell of tuna mixed with chicken permeates the room.

You want it. You are so hungry.

You approach the food gingerly, watching for any change in the man's demeanor, but he goes behind the counter and fiddles with something, ignoring you.

The aroma fills your mouth and nose and washes away any remnants of the pepper spray from before. After a long, stressful day without eating this is exactly what you need.

When the man comes back you pause your munching for a moment, but again he ignores you. He fills white bags with items from the shelves and takes them outside. He comes back and fills more. He does this again and again, on the last trip taking his weapon outside.

By this time you've finished the can and are washing your face, satisfied.

The man returns, squats down and scritches behind your ears. You let him.

"How was that? Hey cat? Was that okay? I've got more of those. Can we be friends now?" his voice is low, soothing.

You rub your head into his hand and he picks you up. He carries you back out into the world and into the car.

The man is resourceful. He is a survivor. And you will stay with him, living a rather pampered and charmed life, despite it being mostly on the road until he encounters another man, also resourceful, also a survivor, who doesn't like cats.

THE END

72

It's dark when you wake up. You are in the girl's lap and you look up and out the windshield. The stars glow bright. Much brighter than in the city. And a crescent moon winks down at you.

The car has slowed considerably, and is crawling up what sounds like a gravel road. The girls are quiet. They've been quiet for a while.

Against the stars, leafy branches silhouette themselves. Finally the car edges up a steep embankment and comes to a rest. The stranger shuts off the car and the sudden silence is intense.

"Hold on a second," the stranger says.

The girl looks over.

"What are we waiting for?"

"I don't know. It's just — things have been crazy. I'm waiting for like, the second shoe to drop or something."

The stranger looks out into the dark woods searchingly.

"Let's do it inside," the girl says. "I'm sick of this car."

The stranger nods.

The three of you leave the car and you inhale the clean air of the country. Your nose pulses as it takes in smells you have never smelt before. All the crap of the city is gone, and as the girl steps away from the car, your nostrils take in remarkably fresh air. Your eyes, already adjusted to the dark, make out the nearby forests, which seem infinitely complex to you, and you are simultaneously apprehensive and entranced. You want to explore them right now. But the girls hustle you into a building.

The stranger turns on a light and it's too bright. You immediately shut your eyes. When they finally adjust, you see that the room is quite large. About as large as the living room back home, with various doors leading off to different rooms.

The girl drops you onto a couch. After a moment of stretching, you drop to the floor.

"You want something to eat?" the stranger says, opening cupboards. "I don't know what we've got left. Usually after we close for the summer we don't leave much."

"Come sit beside me," the girl pats the couch.

The stranger keeps looking through cupboards.

"We should have something," she mutters to herself. Cans, cereal, something here."

"Stop puttering!" the girl gets up and walks over to the stranger.

"Can't help it. I'm stressed!"

"I can help you with that stress," the girl says, and embraces the stranger. She tenses for a moment, her hands hovering, but then she relaxes. They kiss.

As they settle into it, their kissing becomes more intense.

After a few moments, the girls start moving toward a dark doorway. As much as you want to explore, you decide to follow them. The whole day has been completely weird. You miss your house, your backyard, your familiar alley. The places you like to stretch out. Right now you long for the familiar, and the girl is the most familiar thing in your life.

When you enter the room the girls are already in bed and a low bedside lamp is on. You look around for a way to get higher. Finally you jump up onto the bed. You accidentally land on the stranger's foot.

"Whoa!" the stranger says, turning her head around. "Crazy cat."

74

The stranger's foot smells very strong. You bring your nose toward it. Very spicy. Then you turn away. Your real goal is a dresser at the foot of the bed, and you jump up to it now.

The girls make out and slowly get naked.

After a while this gets boring and you close your eyes. Even though you snoozed all day, it wasn't a deep sleep, as the car was moving and shifting the entire time. Here, stretched out on the dresser top, in the dim light, you drift off.

A little while later, you're shocked awake by the girl, screaming.

You open your eyes wide and look around the room.

Then both of the girls laugh.

"Oh that one," the girl whispers, "That last one was pretty amazing."

They go back to kissing.

When you're certain there isn't a threat, you fall asleep again.

Turn to page 42.

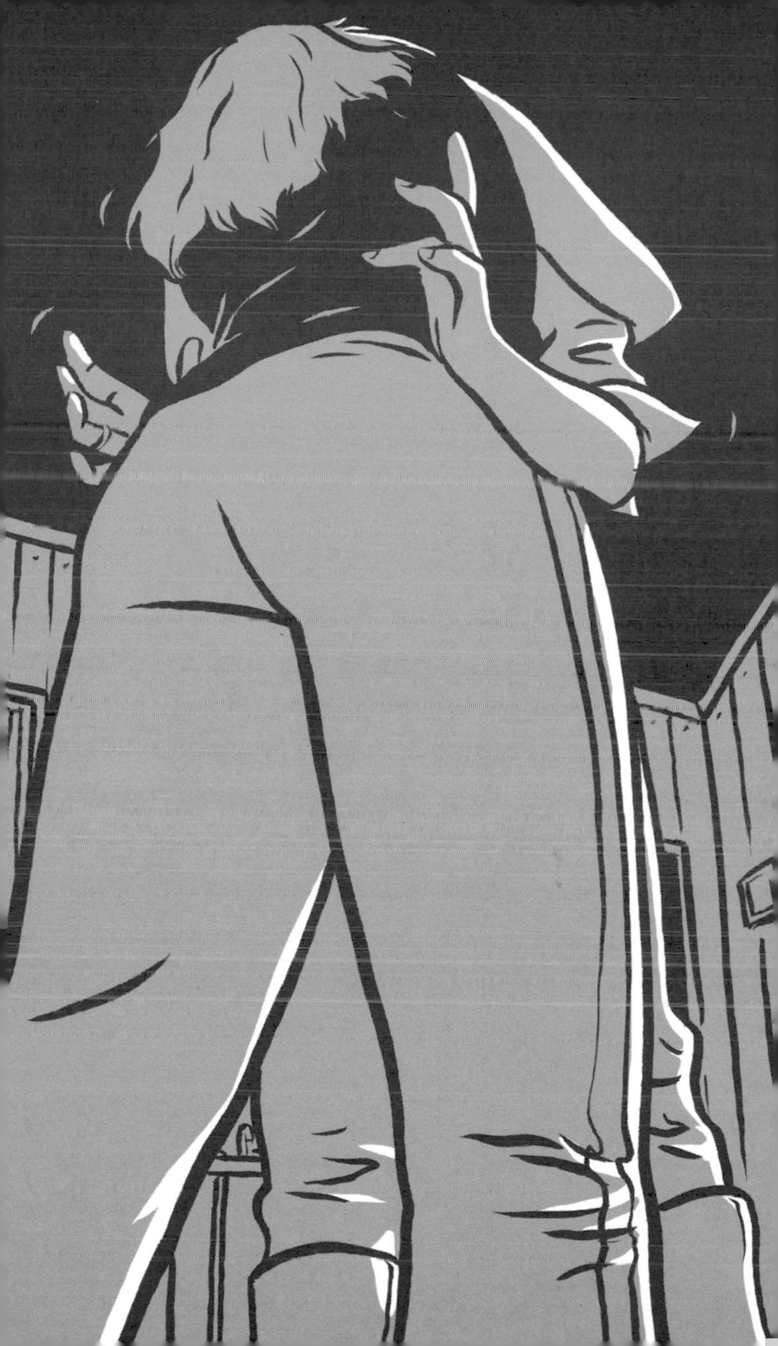

The next time your eyes open you are in a cage. Or rather, a box. Clear plexiglass surrounds you on all sides. You get up slowly, your paws on a clean white plastic floor. You walk over to the plexiglass and bump your nose against it. Little holes let in air.

Beyond the glass, you see a sterile white room with cupboards. There are more empty cells of varying sizes.

On the other side of the room a door opens. A woman and a man in white coats step in.

The man sets up a tripod with a camera on top and aims it at you. The woman has a small white cardboard box in her hand.

"He looks normal," the woman remarks. She gets close to your cage and peers at you.

"What'd you expect?" the man asks.

"I don't know," the woman says. "As an objective viewer I'm not supposed to expect anything."

"Considering the circumstances, though. How could you *not* expect something? Right?"

"His eyes are pretty bloodshot though. He's rather still. Calm, I would say. Unusually so."

"Hold on," the man says. "Stop with your observations until I'm recording."

A small red light appears on the camera.

"Is it on yet?" the woman asks.

"Just a moment. I'm focussing."

The woman checks her watch.

"Alright. Go," the man says.

"Do I need to timestamp this?"

"No. It's on the recording."

"Okay."

The woman steps over to your cage and slides the roof open just a bit. Then, she tips the white box. A

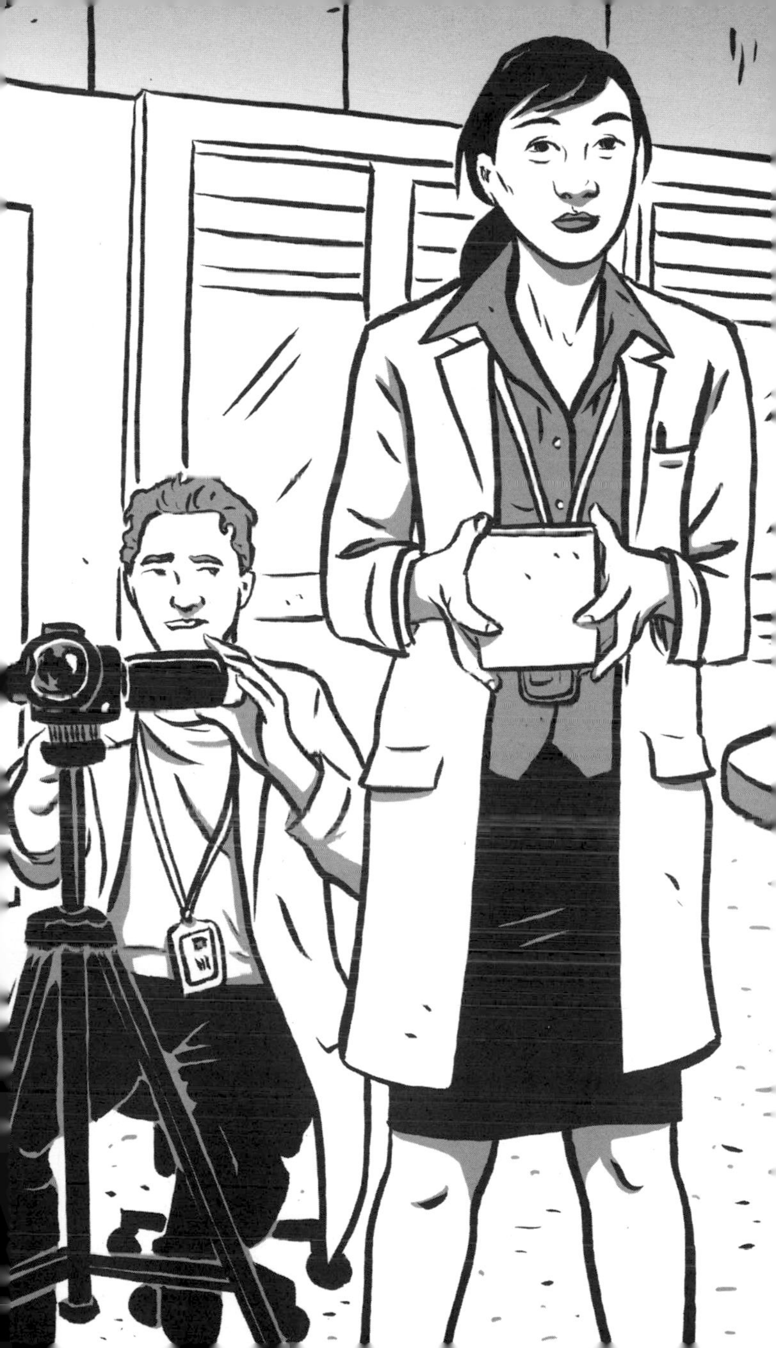

78

small mouse is dropped into your cage!

It hits the ground and immediately looks for cover. It runs into a corner and stands there, trembling.

Its shiny pink eyes stare at you.

If you bite it and turn it into one of your brethren, turn to page 210.

If you decide to let it be for now to see what they will do, turn to page 135.

You know this place. You used to sometimes come here when you were just a regular cat. The large park is home to a swimming pool, a gazebo, tennis courts and a central building. But right now a large chain-link fence surrounds the perimeter, buttressed by large green vehicles and tall supporting poles planted in the grass. In the past, you were wary about going to the park because a huge roadway rims it, and the cars went very fast. But not today.

Today the only vehicle moving is the large green one about to enter the camp.

Men in matching uniforms carry rifles and stand on top of the vehicles, scanning the road.

You gaze at the various bodies littering the street. Some of them are missing their heads. Others are still alive, but barely. You can sense in them little sparks of life.

You need to get inside the camp.

As the large truck enters the main gate, you notice all the sentries turn to watch it.

Now is your chance!

Scurrying along the dead bodies, you make your way to the fence.

Most of it is inaccessible, but there is one place where there is a cat-sized hole because of a particular divot in the ground underneath the fence. You squeeze inside and find yourself in a city of similar green tents.

Farther down, you hear some shouting.

Curious, you move down the line of tents and see a separate fenced-in area. Green uniformed men and women surround it. A man, completely naked, a pile of clothes at his feet, yells at them.

"No, I got this the other day!" He taps at his

shoulder, where part of his skin is missing. "Before whatever's been happening! I'm not infected! It was an accident in the garage where I work!"

"Sir, please put your clothes back on."

"No! You can't send me back out there!" The naked man sits down on the flattened grass. "I deserve protection. You're the army aren't you? Well you work for *me!* I pay my taxes. I'm *entitled* to protection!"

"Sir, put your clothes back on please."

The naked man just shakes his head.

"Sir, we'll send you out there without your clothes," one of the uniforms says.

The man frowns, then stands.

"You would, wouldn't you? You bastards."

The man begins to put on his clothes.

Suddenly, a scream.

A woman comes running over to the fence from inside the camp.

"Jack!" she says, putting her fingers into the chain-link.

"Ma'am, stay back!" A soldier chasing her grabs her around the waist and pulls her back from the fence. He looks at the other soldiers. "Sorry," he says sheepishly, "She ran from the dining area."

"Hey! Don't touch her!" the man yells. He drops his clothes and presses against the fence. "Riley! I'm here!"

"Uncle Jack!" the woman reaches out to the man.

"They won't let me in," the man says. "They think I'm infected."

The woman looks at the soldiers. "What's wrong with you?! Let him in!"

"Ma'am, get back to the dining area."

A couple soldiers begin to drag the woman away.

"No! No!"

She is screaming the whole time. The man yells at them. Finally it's quiet again.

The man stands, half-naked, weeping, holding his shirt in his hands.

The gate opens and the man walks out.

"Tell my neice that I love her," he tells the soldiers. "You probably won't, but if there's any shred of humanity left in you, you'll tell her."

The man stands just outside the gates, looking lost.

"Good luck sir," a soldier says.

The man calls back over his shoulder: "Assholes."

He is an easy target. You consider following him.

If you decide to exit the camp and follow the man, turn to page 82.

If you decide instead that you want to find a quieter area, turn to page 85.

There is, however, the whiff of food in the air. Though your tastes don't align with your previous diet as a cat, you know that where there is food, there is people. If you want to bring your new particular brand of love to the people, turn to page 84.

Backtracking, you exit the camp and trot along the side of the fence toward the half-naked man. By the time you reach him, he has his T-shirt back on. He faces a soldier standing just on the other side of the fence.

"Look," the man says. "If you're so convinced that I'm infected, why don't you just shoot me? Shoot me right now. Take me out of my misery."

"Sir, we're *not* sure. But we can't take the chance."

"Then shoot me now!" The man gestures down the street. "I'm not going to survive out there! It'll be an act of kindness!"

"I can't sir."

"You've been shooting folks all day! I've watched you!"

"I have my orders sir. Not unless and until you turn. I can't. Until then, it's murder."

The man is silent for a second.

"How's Riley? How's my neice doing?"

"She's been sedated for her protection."

The man sighs, then sits down heavily on the sidewalk. He sighs again.

"Sir, you can't stay here. You'll risk getting targeted by our snipers."

The man looks him in the eyes.

"Good," he says, simply.

Now is your chance. You look at the man's bare arm.

But wait.

No. You are beginning to sense the man. He is changing. He is becoming one of you. You don't *need* to bring your love to him. He *already* is full of love.

Then he notices you. He takes a deep breath.

"Hey kitty."

The soldier frowns. "Where?!" he demands, sharply.

The man holds his arms out and you go to him.

"Sir!" the soldier barks, lifting his gun. "Stay away from the cat! I can't protect you!"

The man gives the soldier a dirty look.

"Fuck you!"

Then the man lifts you into his arms and hugs you. You can feel from the laboured breathing in his chest and the change in his scent that he is joining your collective.

"Sir, let go of the cat!"

The man gets to his feet and begins to walk away from the camp.

"Heh, hah," the man wheezes.

"Sir! Drop the cat!" the soldier warns.

The man lifts one arm and gives the middle finger as he walks.

Then the man stumbles and drops you.

He turns and pants at the soldier.

He starts walking back to the camp.

"Sir!" the soldier warns, and fires his rifle.

He misses.

But the second shot does not.

The man's head explodes in a shower of gore.

His body drops on top of you.

Crushed, you are unable to get free.

You try to release yourself for the next day and a half before the collective decides to cut its loss and let you go. It is the most painful, wrenching feeling when they leave you to die by yourself, as your self.

THE END

84

You follow your nose to a clearing in the tents. A crowd of people sit at plastic picnic tables, eating. Their voices are terse and restrained. You don't know what they're saying, but you know how they're saying it.

On one side, food is being served up in enormous pots. A plastic pallet full of bottled water is torn open and half the bottles are dispersed amongst the people there. Piles of luggage are stacked on the other side.

People eat off paper plates, eating with plastic utensils.

Suddenly, a motion on your right. It's a girl.

She's a younger human. She bends down and puts her plate on the ground in front of you.

"Kitty!" she squeals, delighted.

The motion is familiar. You smell the food. A stew of some kind. It smells all wrong now. In the past you would have been curious. Human food is not so fascinating now.

You look at the little girl. You look at her wrist. You are momentarily confused. You used to be governed primarily by food, but now it's taken a secondary priority, now that you know about the collective, and their overwhelming love for you, and their desire to spread that overwhelming love to the world, and how you can do it by biting this girl's wrist.

If you decide to bite the girl, chomp down on page 158.

If instead you retreat, and explore elsewhere, escape to page 95.

Venturing further into the nest of tents, you encounter even larger ones. You see a slit in the side of one and you poke your head in.

You see two cots set up, one on either side. Both occupied. The soft sounds of snoring men fill the space.

One of the men has his arm hanging down to the ground.

You move over to it and bite it!

The man wakes, then screams!

The other man jumps awake and pulls a gun out from underneath his pillow. He fires it at you!

You run!

You dash along the line of tents.

The sound of panicked voices.

"Cat! There's a cat in here! It's biting!"

Distantly, an alarm whines.

Now you hear something else. Something very familiar.

A chorus of barks.

There are *dogs* here.

They'll be coming for you.

Suddenly, a soldier rounds a bend and sees you. He fires his gun!

You duck around a corner and run the other way.

A dog has just spotted you!

You deke down a third path and head back into the tent city with the dog hot on your scent.

Then you hear a voice.

"Marv! Heel! Heel!"

Curious, you look back.

The dog stares back from a distance. A woman in uniform stands behind him. The dog barks, but makes no move to chase you.

Why did it stop?

As you stare, a black bag is slipped over your head! A drawstring tightens it around your neck.

You howl, resisting, but you are pulled roughly into a larger canvas bag, then lifted into the air.

You hear a voice.

"Got him! Thanks for flushing him out. Get him to the lab. They were looking for a sample."

Moments later, you are put on a truck. You hear its grumbling engine.

Despite your discomfort, you can't do anything, so the collective shuts you down, and lets your body sleep.

Turn to page 76.

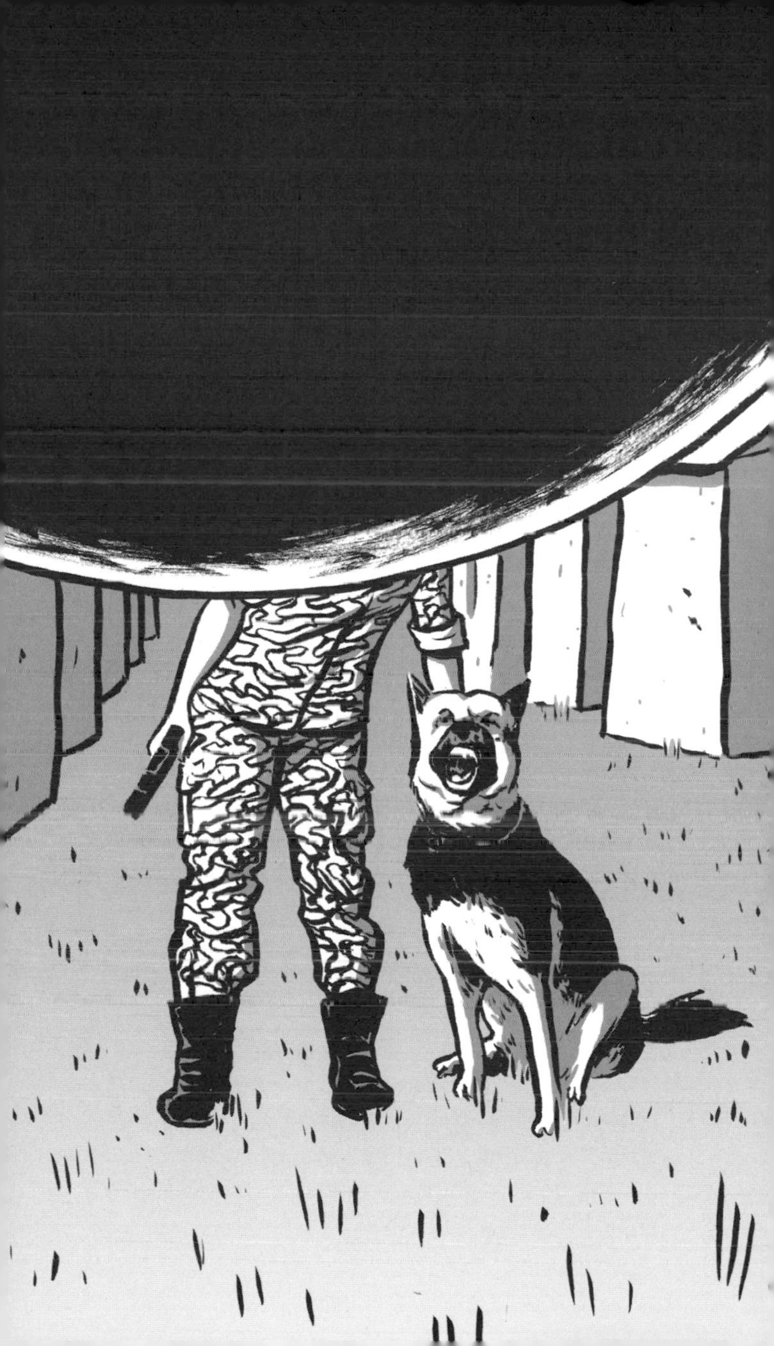

88

You follow the stranger outside. She stands for a moment on the porch, her hands on the railing.

"It was right to come here," she nods to herself. "This was smart."

You jump off the porch and onto the grass.

"Don't go far, kitten," the stranger says to you. The cabin is built on a gentle slope, and stiff pilings keep the building level.

The stranger clambers off the porch and immediately drops down onto the grass. On her belly she shuffles into the crawlspace under the cabin. You watch her, venturing into the space yourself. What is she doing?

In the dark recess of the crawlspace, the stranger unlocks a padlock, and opens a small wood door. Then she pushes aside some junk and pulls out a long, black case.

You wonder if you can get into that space.

As if reading your mind, the stranger looks at you, "Don't — even think about it, kitten." Once the case is pulled out, she shuts the door immediately, and puts the padlock back on.

Now she backs out from under the cabin and, with another key, opens up the case.

Inside is a long, dark metal tube. You step close and smell it. The scent of oil emanates from it.

The stranger pulls out and attaches the metal part to a wooden stock. Then, bringing one end to her shoulder and the other up into the air, she closes one eye and makes noises with her mouth.

"Boom!" she whispers, and raises the end of the tube slightly, before bringing it back down.

Now you're getting bored. You decide to explore. Maybe find something to eat.

Turning to the woods, you hear distant flowing water from the left, but birds are chirping to the right, by some bushes.

Head to the water on page 43.

If you'd rather investigate the birds, turn to page 97.

You decide to head back down to the street, but first you take in the view. From this vantage point you have a lovely vista of other rooftops stretching out to the horizon. You feel like a much bigger cat. Imagine if all this was your territory!

Then you look down at the body on the ground several floors below. A gentle breeze rustles his long blonde hair. A small pool of blood forms around his head, trapping some of the hairs, like flies in honey.

A small movement catches your attention. The tiniest dog appears from behind some garbage cans and staggers over to the body. The dog is infected. What's worse, it's one of those tiny yappy dogs that let out a torrent of sharp barks at the slightest provocation. You normally dislike and distrust dogs, but you might hate those the most.

The dog steps into the man's bloodied hair, then, in one swift movement leaps on his face! He chews on the man's lips. Blood spurts and drools down the man's chin. An urgent, unearthly sound comes out of the dog, midway between a pant and a grunt.

Finally it jumps down, trailing bloodied paw prints as it trots away.

The man is now missing his nose.

A small bloody misshapen hole is all that's left.

Desecrated and dessicated bodies are not unfamiliar. You've done your own share of mauling and mutilating, but you have never seen a human become a victim. All your life humans have been the ones who've had all the power. The power to feed you. The power to move you around. The power to let you in or out of rooms. Everything is changing and you are not sure how to handle it.

There's that sound again.

You look down for the dog but it's gone.

Wait, it's not the dog making the sound — it's the man!

The bloody blonde-haired man jerks on the ground, turns, makes his way to his knees, then rises to his feet.

You've seen enough. You turn around and move over to the doorway. You look at the corpse holding the door open warily. Is it going to come back to life too?

Then, from the darkness inside the doorway, you see a pair of eyes.

They are so familiar.

You have gazed into them for many hours.

"Heh, heh," the owner of the eyes says.

You stop. You don't move as your girlfriend steps out into the light. She is ragged and wretched, her fur matted and bloodied. One of her ears is a bloodied stump. Long gashes trench her flesh.

Momentarily she is drawn to the man's body, but returns her focus to you.

You step back.

Your heart is torn — you are delighted she's still alive, but sad that this has happened to her.

She moves closer and you turn, run a few steps, then turn back around to look at her.

This repeats until you are almost out of roof.

You could try to run around her. You are not sure if she is speedy enough to cut you off.

But part of you doesn't *want* to outrun her. You are tired of running. Seems like this whole day has been about running.

In your moment of hesitation, she is suddenly on you! The faint echo of her former beautiful scent

92

clings to her fur and you inhale it.

You don't exhale.

Even as her teeth wrench into your neck you stubbornly hold your breath. You want her scent in your lungs forever.

You hold on. You hold on.

She is tearing your flesh.

Finally, as you lose consciousness you relax and let her go.

Turn to page 25.

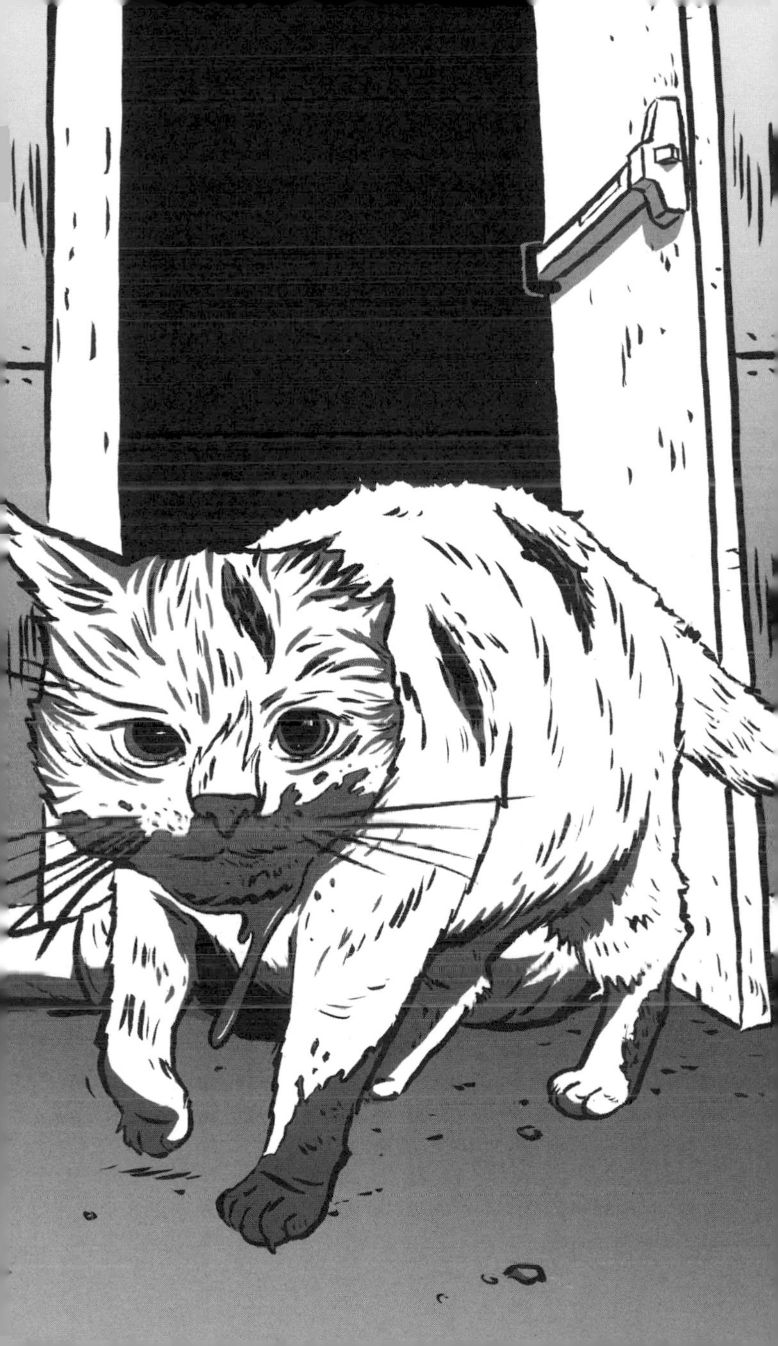

Neither you nor your girlfriend move as the man on top of the truck looks around.

Then, from an alley across the street, you hear quiet panting. Two shadows step out into the light.

Like a pigeon's swivelling head, the man sees them immediately and turns his rifle toward them.

"Eyes on two Zs," the man says. "Alley."

The two infected, attracted by the man's voice, move forward toward the truck.

The man holds his gun a little tighter — doesn't take his eyes off them.

"Am I clear to engage?" the man asks.

"Are you certain?" a voice crackles from the small speaker attached to the man's clothes.

"I'm certain, sir."

"Weapons free."

The man aims carefully, and shoots the heads off the two infected.

"Zone 15. Two Zs down,' the man reports.

"Roger. Continue on your route."

The green truck rumbles into movement and continues along the street.

You look over at your girlfriend. She still has blood on her face from when she was mauling the pigeons. You lick her face, licking the blood off. She licks your face and fur in turn, cleaning off any stray drops.

It's a nice moment of quiet after a crazy day.

Keeping to the underside of cars and the cover of bushes, you and your girlfriend wander away in the opposite direction of the green truck.

Turn to page 65.

Seeing one tent that is larger than the others, you decide to have a look.

When you enter, you keep to the edges. You are wary. You don't want to be noticed unless you can use it to your advantage. There are three cots in this tent, and you immediately move underneath one.

A tall man in a grey suit stands talking to another man in a green uniform. At the far end, a little girl has a suitcase open on a cot. She is rummaging through it.

"So where's my wife?" the grey suit asks.

"She's en route to the boat already," the uniform replies.

"How are *we* getting there?"

"You and the other VIPs are being flown to an island on the tip of the mainland. There's no infection there. It's a temporary staging area to refuel. From there, we'll get you to Cuba. Island countries seem to be clean for now. From Cuba, we'll settle you on a fleet of cruise ships where we'll regroup."

"Dad, what's happening?" the girl asks.

"Cupcake, just keep packing your stuff," grey suit says to the girl. Then, to the uniform, "When are we leaving?"

"Twenty minutes soon enough for you? I'll send someone to escort you to the helipad."

"Don't bother. My daughter and I know where it is. Thank you."

Grey suit shakes the uniform's hand, and the man leaves.

"C'mon Cupcake, we leave in twenty."

"I can't find Mookie."

The grey suit sighs.

"We'll have to leave without him."

The girl's face crumples.

96

"I need to find Mookie!"

"Well, where do you think you could have left him?"

"I don't know!"

The grey suit looks around the tent.

"Did you have him last night?"

"Well, yah."

"We were in a different tent last night..." the grey suit scratches his chin. "Hold on, I'll go look for him. Don't go anywhere."

The grey suit leaves the tent. The girl keeps looking through her suitcase. Then she abruptly leaves the tent.

"Wait! Dad!"

You are getting tired of running around. Her suitcase seems like a nice cozy place to take a rest. If you slip into the girl's suitcase, turn to page 114.

If, however, you still want to explore the other tents, go for it on page 85.

You slow as you approach the leafy bush and the birds inside.

You don't want to alarm them unduly. They flit from branch to branch. Their activity reminds you of a stormcloud you once saw on a particularly humid day — little lightning flashes erupted here and there inside, illuminating localized sections of the cloud, so quiet you didn't hear any accompanying thunder.

And quiet is how you move now.

But all of a sudden they see you.

A couple birds fly off deeper into the woods, but one comes right at you!

Startled, you step back as it veers into the grass in front of your face.

One wing flaps stupidly as it chirps at you.

It's almost as if it forgot how to fly.

"Chirrr-up!" the bird screams at you.

This is too weird. A bird has never made that sound before. Not even when you've been ripping its wings off. And they make really intense noises as you rip their wings off.

You go over and claw at its wing, to get it to stop.

It does.

Good. That's more familiar.

Then the bird erupts in a violent explosion of flapping and writhing and you grab at it with your other paw! It keeps struggling and you bite down on it. But it manages to squirm free. Amazing. This bird is a fighter.

Miraculously, the bird gets loose. As you rear up to smother it, it pecks you in the belly!

You cover it with your body but it continues to struggle.

You let it go. This is too much.

98

Normally when you let a bird go, it gets as far away as possible. But this one keeps coming at you. Flying awkwardly, hopping, rolling.

You don't like this at all.

You run.

Head back to the cabin on page 118.

You step on the prickly metal steps and slowly begin your ascent. Right behind, your girlfriend follows.

There are a few windows on the way, and curious, you look in.

Someone is drinking out of a long bottle in one room. In another, two men are watching television, arms around each other. The last is a window that is slightly open with a screen. You bring your nose close to it. Cooking smells drift out.

You stop for a second, trying to discern exactly what is being cooked, but your girlfriend moves past you impatiently to the roof.

You follow.

At the top, you both find a beautiful surprise.

A structure stands.

You have never seen such a marvellous thing.

Made of wood and wire, it's a cage full of birds!

What's it doing here?

You and your girlfriend wander over, mesmerized.

Pigeons of various shades flit nervously inside. Brown, grey and black wings flutter in a spectacle as the nervous birds utter coos.

You feel so proud that you are able to bring your girlfriend up here, that you are showing her a good time.

She goes up to the wire screen and puts her paw on it. The wires are spaced quite close together, so she's unable to put her paw fully inside. The birds, disturbed, move away from her.

You peer closely at the latch holding the pigeon coop door closed.

It's a single metal hook. It looks a little like the bathroom door hook at home.

100

Can you open it?

The birds dance in front of you. They are trying to hide their fear, but you see it clearly.

Do you try to open the coop? Turn to page 129.

Or, if you decide to leave it well enough alone, turn to page 142.

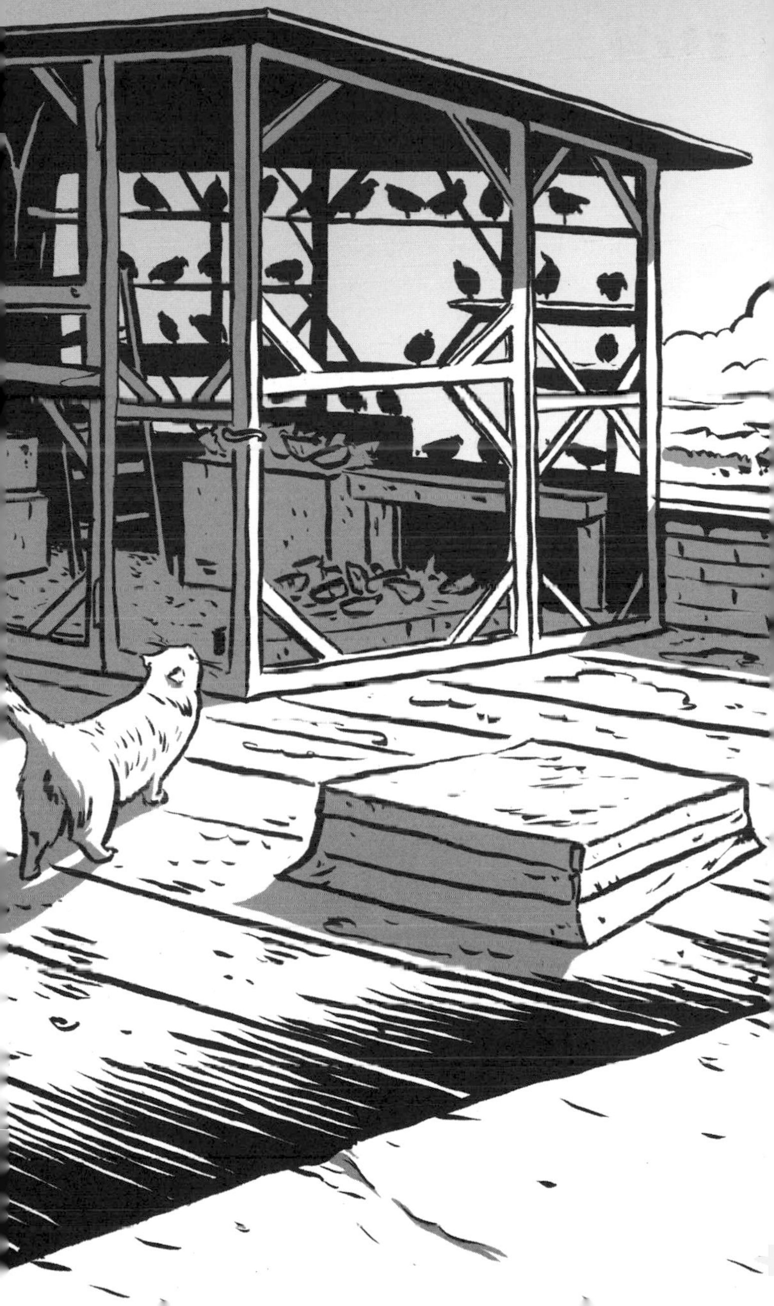

You bound into the back of the minivan alongside your girlfriend. It's filled with boxes, sleeping bags and a few small suitcases. There are plenty of places to hide.

Just as the two of you tuck into a shadow beside a bag you hear the people coming back.

"C'mon kids, don't dawdle," the woman says. Her voice is sharp and prickly, like a rosebush.

The two girls step into the minivan and you feel the floor shift slightly as they get into their seats.

"Where are we goin'?" one of the kids asks. She seems to be the youngest person there.

"We're going to dad's work," the woman says, closing a sliding door.

"Is dad there?"

"Yes, your father's there."

"Why don't we stay here? Why can't he come home?"

"We can't — " the woman starts, then stops. "We can't defend ourselves here," she says. "There are some things at the store that can help us."

Once everyone is settled, the woman starts the vehicle and backs it slowly out into the street.

"What sort of things?"

"Just — there's safety equipment."

"What sort of safety equipment?"

"Katie, honey," the woman sighs. "Let me drive."

The minivan sets off through the night and the hum of it soothes you.

Then a shock! One of the girls puts her hand on your back!

She inhales sharply, but the sound is lost in the sound of the vehicle.

You look up and she peers at you. Then she notices your girlfriend, tucked beside you.

"Katie, what is it?" the other girl asks.

"I'm just — I'm just looking for toys."

"Girls, I told you," the woman calls back. "You can only bring along *two* toys. And that's it. Besides, there's some toys at the store."

"I know Mom," the girl says, "I'm just looking."

The woman turns on the radio but it's mostly just static. Finally she gets a signal. It's pretty nice.

"Classical," the woman says. "Figures. I hate classical."

The girl taps her older sister on the shoulder and puts her fingers to her lips. The older girl scowls at her then sees us. A huge grin breaks out on her face as well.

The trip is quite long.

Occasionally the little girl will turn around again, stroke you and your girlfriend, then settle back down again.

Once, the woman said sharply, "Girls, cover your eyes!"

"Why, Mom?"

"Just do what I say! God!"

And the girls dutifully covered their eyes while the woman accelerated.

"Can we look now Mom?" the older girl asked, hands still up to her face.

"Yes, I think it's okay now."

"What was it?"

"I'll — I'll tell you later. When we get to the store. Okay?"

Finally the car slows and enters a parking lot. It's completely dark outside by now.

You look out the window and see a number of

storefronts lined up next to each other. Nothing is familiar.

The woman steers the vehicle so its lights shine on the store closest. A black metal gate covers the front door and the windows. It's dark inside.

"Dad's here? It looks closed," the little girl says.

"He's meeting us here," the woman says. She drives the minivan around the side of the store, then stops behind it.

"Why are we going in the back way?" the older girl asks.

"Girls just — please," the woman shuts the car off and rubs her temples. "Just do as I say?"

There's something in the woman's voice you don't like.

The girls must have sensed it too because they are silent for a moment. Then the older girl says, "Okay, Mom."

The woman gets out of the car slowly. The interior light comes on and you and your girlfriend wince at the sudden brightness.

"Don't slam the doors," the woman calls into the car. She goes over to the store and unlocks the back door, then pops open the rear door of the minivan.

"Help me carry things in," she whispers. She grabs a box and disappears inside the store.

"Do you think we can keep them?" the younger one asks.

"I don't know. You know Dad's allergic."

"Let's just — " the younger girl unzips a backpack and grabs you. You resist for a moment, but the older girl helps her wrestle you into it. You struggle at first, but it's actually kind of nice in there. There are soft pillowy things inside that have very strong scents.

Your girlfriend soon follows, and it's rather cosy. Then the top is zipped up and the girls leave the car.

"What are you girls doing?" the woman's voice, ringed with tension says.

"Sorry Mom."

"Help me get these things inside!"

You and your girlfriend are carried for a bit and then are dumped onto a floor. The surface is warm and soft through the fabric of the bag, so you assume it's carpet underneath rather than tiles.

Squished warmly together like this, your girlfriend begins to purr. You purr back and lick behind her ear. You close your eyes and wish you could be squished here against your girlfriend forever. This has been a day of uncertainty, but there is nothing uncertain about this quiet wish in your heart.

But things always change. And it's not always up to you.

You hear the back door close, and the humans finally stop talking in whispers.

"Can we turn on the lights?"

"No, we shouldn't," the woman responds. "Just use your flashlights, girls."

"How will Dad know we're here?"

"He'll know," the woman says. "Okay. You girls get squared away. Unroll your sleeping bags. I'm going downstairs for a second. Behave."

"Okay Mom."

A moment later, you feel yourself swinging in mid-air as the backpack is lifted, then put down again. The top is unzipped and the younger girl looks in at you.

"Aww, look at them. So cute!"

A bright light shines in at you and you immediately close your eyes and look away.

"Katie don't shine the light *right* in their faces!"

The light abruptly disappears.

"Mom's coming back!" the older girl whispers.

"Girls, come here!" the woman says.

The backpack falls onto its side and you find yourself staring at carpet.

You hear the girls pad over to the woman.

"What is that?" the older girl asks. "Is that a gun?"

"You're not to touch this," the woman states sternly. "Do you hear me? Never. Ever. Now, I know you might be curious, so I'm going to show it to you right now. Okay? Katie, come here and shine your light on it."

Your girlfriend wiggles free of the bag and emerges onto the carpet. You kind of want to stay in the bag, but your curiousity compels you to leave as well.

Tall shelves tower around you on either side. You look down the aisle. More shelves stand farther down. You sniff at the array of items on the shelves. Nothing smells even remotely like food.

Suddenly there's a noise near the front window.

The woman stops her demonstration.

"Quiet girls."

You watch as the woman walks to the front of the store and peers out the window. Just outside, a metal grate hangs. A couple of streetlights at the entrance to the parking lot cast their pale light into the dark store.

"What is it Mom?" one of the girls whispers.

"I don't know. Be quiet."

The woman goes over to the front door and unlocks it, then opens it.

"Don't Mom!" the older girl calls.

The woman looks back.

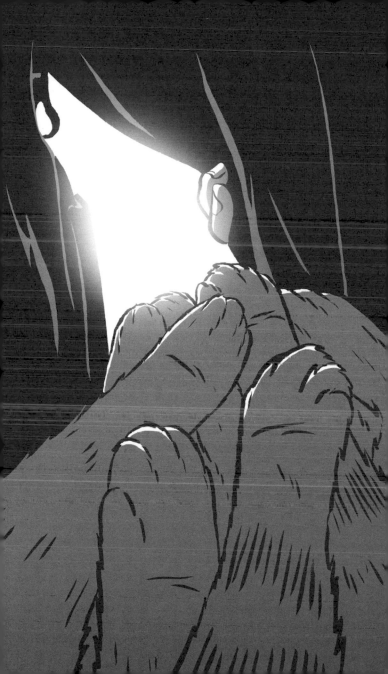

108

"It's okay, we have the security gate. We're safe."

Your girlfriend creeps up toward the woman. With the front door open, the cool night air wafts into the stuffy store. Your nose twitches at the scents the air carries.

The woman opens the front door and holds it open with her back foot. She moves her head to the metal gate and looks around.

Suddenly, your girlfriend runs past the woman and out the bottom of the gate!

"Jesus Christ!" the woman yells, startled.

"Don't shoot it!" the girls chorus, behind you.

If you follow your girlfriend outside, gallop to page 163.

If instead, you stay right where you are, dig in on page 159.

You don't follow your girlfriend. You don't want to be trapped inside the minivan.

Your girlfriend's face appears at the door. She looks at you. Meows.

You don't want to do this.

Suddenly, the door to the house opens again. Your girlfriend's face disappears into the vehicle. You run over and hide behind a tree. It is largely shadowed, so you feel pretty safe.

"C'mon kids, get in the car," the woman says.

You watch as two small girls clamber in. The woman goes around back and shuts the doors there, then climbs in herself.

You think about your girlfriend. Now she's trapped. The minivan starts up with a roar. Its lights flash, then it backs out into the street.

You follow it with your eyes as it moves down to the intersection, then rounds the corner. Then it's gone.

Your girlfriend is gone.

You sit on the driveway for a bit.

You gaze up at the deep blue sky, now etched with thin clouds.

You see some lights at the end of the street!

Maybe they are coming back?

But the lights continue smoothly along, never stopping. It wasn't them.

Pretty soon it's dark, and cold, and quiet.

You can see the faintest condensation of your breath as you breathe. There's nowhere to go.

You wander over to the next house over. You sit on its porch.

This doesn't seem to be anyone's territory. In fact, this whole area is pretty scentless. Random trees and bushes have markings, of course, but the smells are diffused.

You startle when the door to the house opens, jumping down to the grass and hiding under a bush.

You watch as an old woman comes out in a dark black rolling chair.

She has a calmness about her that you immediately sense.

"I saw you," she calls out. "These eyes might be old, but they see everything." The woman makes chucking noises with her tongue, like a chipmunk.

You stand in the grass, staring at her.

"Are you hungry? I have some food for you."

The woman rolls back into the house, leaving the front door open.

You creep back over to the porch. You can hear the woman inside, opening cupboards. Then you hear a very distinctive noise. You love that noise. *A can is being opened!*

You venture into the house.

In the middle of the kitchen floor sits an open can of tuna. You go over to it. Its smell is overwhelming. You are so hungry. You become aware of the woman sitting in her chair in a corner. She smiles at you.

"Go ahead," she urges.

You bring your face to the food and lick the thick, salty brine. Your mouth immediately waters and you dig in. It's not the canned food that you're used to, but in some ways this is better. It's less of a mishmash of various meats. It's a little cleaner — more like the taste of actual animals.

"Meals on Wheels didn't come today. Can't get a hold of my son — though that's nothing new. You're the only visitor I've had all day."

After finishing your meal, you fall asleep on the couch after licking yourself clean.

Later, you wake up in the middle of the night to hear the woman struggle out of her chair and into a bed in the corner of the living room. Then you go back to sleep.

Some hours pass before you are roused again. Something woke you, but you're not sure what. That's when the front door opens and a young man steps in. He pauses when he sees you, but does not make a noise. He looks over at the woman, sleeping, snoring, then kicks his shoes off.

You go over to smell his shoes. The odour is astonishing. He's been sweating a lot. As he walks upstairs his socks practically leave steaming footprints. You follow him.

The man turns the light on in a large room. Nothing here has been touched in a long time. A thin layer of dust covers most things.

When you walk into the room he shoots you a look, then goes back to what he's doing. You jump up onto the bed and watch him.

The man goes over to a dresser in a corner, opens it, and begins putting small metal things into his pockets. He opens a box and examines small chains and rings. He puts everything into his pockets.

When he's done, he comes over to you and gives you his hand. You sniff at his fingers. You smell smoke. And something sweeter. Like burned flowers. The man strokes your ears then turns off the light and goes back downstairs. You drop down to the floor and follow.

The man makes a beeline to his shoes.

"What did you take?" the woman says. She is sitting up in her bed.

"Mom!" the man is startled to see her up.

"My jewelery," she says flatly. "I would have left it to you — you know that," the woman says.

"I need it *now*, Mom," the man says.

"Alec, what's going on out there?"

The man puts on his shoes.

"What's this cat doing in here anyway? It could be infected, Mom."

"If it were, and it infected me, then maybe I could walk again."

"It doesn't work like that Mom."

"How does it work then? Huh? Tell me."

The man doesn't answer her. He just looks at her for a moment, then leaves.

"Hey!" she screams after him. "Hey!"

The door closes and you can hear him walk quickly away.

The woman is shaking, breathing hard. She closes her eyes then falls back onto the bed.

It takes her a long time to go back to sleep, but she does, and you do too.

In the morning, she gets into her chair and rolls out onto the porch and down a small ramp that extends to her driveway. When she is on the street, she looks back at the house. You stand on the grass. Where is she going?

"C'mon kitty." The woman pats her lap.

With initial trepidation, you jump up onto her lap. When she first pushes the stick, and the chair starts rolling, you are scared. But after a while you kind of like it.

"I've never really gone all the way to Joseph Street in my chair like this. But I should have enough of a charge."

Ahead of you, a man stands beside a car. The woman looks at him warily. He is one of the infected, and, seeing her, staggers over.

Deftly, the woman steers her chair to avoid him. The combination of his slow movements, and her nimbleness allow her to deke past the man. He follows her for a long time, but he is too slow and the chair is too fast. Eventually he is just a dot in the distance behind you.

But the chair starts to slow. Then it stops.

"Oh no," the woman says. She turns her head, sees the man. The figure gets bigger.

"Get out of here kitty," she says. You look up at the woman. Her face is crumpling.

"Oh god there's more of them!" The woman keeps swivelling her head. You take a look around too. Coming out of the houses, the backyards, more of the infected. All zeroing in.

The man who you had left behind is suddenly terrifyingly close. The woman grabs you and throws you off her lap just as the man bends down and bites her neck.

"Ah!" the woman cries. Munching noises as he keeps at her.

Then a pair of grimy hands grabs you!

And soon you join the melody of munching.

Your flesh and fur tearing is the worst sound in the world.

Blessedly, you black out.

Turn to page 25.

You jump up onto the cot and peer into the suitcase. A bunch of clothes sit inside, alongside some books, some toys. Everything smells just a little too sweet.

The collective is eager for you to stow away in the suitcase. They seem to know something you don't. Or rather, they have a hunch about something they want you to test. You don't know how they know this, or feel this — all you know is that they have a collective feeling about what they'd like you to do, and you are doing it.

You step gingerly into the case and burrow under a sweater.

It's very cozy.

You're reminded of your former life, when you would nuzzle into the caves made by comforters and duvets. Warm as warm could be. You've been cold for a while now, though the love of collective is fiery on the inside.

"I told you to stay here! Didn't I?" the grey suit says. The voices get stronger as they re-enter the tent.

"I thought I could help!"

The grey suit sighs.

"Put Mookie away and let's go. We don't have much time."

Something soft falls on you, and then all light is extinguished.

You hear a zip close, and then the case is yanked into the air.

"Hurry hon."

"It's heavy! Mookie's heavy!"

"Here, let me take it."

The case is jolted to the side and then you are swinging through the air.

"Mookie *is* heavy," the grey suit grunts. "I thought I told you to take *only* the necessary clothes! Not *all* of them!"

"I *did!*"

"I've heard *that* before."

After a considerable walk, finally you are set down again.

"Where are we going, Dad?"

"We're going to meet Mum. But it's a bit of a trip. So you might as well relax. Try to sleep if you can. It's going to be very loud, so put in these earplugs if you like."

You hear a slow whine that grows into a loud roar. You are insulated somewhat by the sweaters and the suitcase, however.

You decide to withdraw for a bit.

When you close your eyes, it's quite marvellous. The collective is right there with you. It's as if every single member is a small stream, but you all flow into a larger ocean, and are made powerful by that.

You find that you can see things through other members' eyes. Suddenly you have a vision of a helicopter from the point of view of a bird. This bird has been following you. With absolute certainty you know that you are inside that helicopter, inside a suitcase.

You move around some more. You are in your old backyard! You see your cat door! You are a squirrel — scouting the neighbourhood for the as-yet unloved.

It is heady and delirious and you spend an indeterminate amount of time doing this before you decide to return to your cat body and your cat consciousness.

Swing. Swing. Swing. Thud.

The suitcase falls on the ground and you are jolted rudely back.

"This is your cabin, sir," a young man says.

"Thanks," grey suit replies.

"*Now* can I get Mookie out?"

"Alright, cupcake."

The suitcase is pushed over on its side and you hear a zip — then it's bright. A large hand lifts a plush toy off of you. You see the girl, and beyond her, a small room.

"Oh!" the girl stares at you. "*Dad!*"

The grey suit is standing by the door of the cabin, looking out. He turns.

"What is it?"

"There's a *cat* here!"

You bite the girl's wrist! She screams!

"What the fuck?!" The grey suit runs over.

You dash between his legs and out the door. You find yourself in a long corridor and start moving down it.

"Hey! Hey! I need help here!" the grey suit yells.

More doors open on either side. People rush out. A man steps out into the hall between you and the grey suit.

"What's the matter?" he asks.

You ravish his ankle.

"Ah!" he screams! He tries to kick you off and loses his balance. He falls on his ass.

You let go and run into his room.

"You see *that?* It's a cat! It might be infected!" grey suit yells.

A woman appears by the fallen man's side.

"Eric! What happened? Are you okay?"

"We have a situation. Call in a code white. It's a cat."

The woman pulls a radio from her pocket and pushes a button. You leap on her forearm!

"Ah!"

"There it is!"

Grey suit runs over and tries to kick you, but he misses and falls!

Immediately you pounce on the man's face and tear into his lips.

This is *great*.

Blood spurts into your eyes and nose and you feel the love flowing back and forth from you into the man and into the other people in the corridor. Inside you, the collective is cheering you on. They are so pleased with you. They weren't sure they could get here. This ship, so far out into the ocean. The fish were unable to penetrate the hull. The birds were unable to fly out this far.

But for you — beautiful stowaway — love might not have reached this last human bastion of the unloved and unconnected.

Is this
THE END
or merely the *beginning?*

118

The trip back to the cabin is difficult. It's not far, but you are having trouble keeping awake and alert. Woozy, the numerous trees easily confuse you.

Furthermore, the wound on your belly is beginning to throb. But at the same time, a kind of soothing salve is being released from the point of contact, leaving you a little high.

Finally you stumble up the embankment and over onto the porch. Your head bumps into the door. You wish you were home, with your cat door, so you didn't have to beg to be let in.

Inside you can hear the girls talking.

You scratch at the door.

Can they hear you?

The conversation stops. They're coming. You hear footsteps and feel vibrations on the floor.

"Hey baby," the girl opens the door and reaches for you.

"Hey *hey!*" the stranger warns. "Check him!"

The girl sighs. "Look!" she rubs your head, "He's not a fucking zombie! No blood dripping down his chin!"

"*Check* him!"

The girl bends down and holds your head between her hands. You blink at her. You need to pass out, you think. She massages your head, and strokes you from head to tail. She runs her hands down your paws and hind legs. She turns to the stranger.

"Nothing, see?"

The stranger frowns and bends close.

"Give him here."

"Fine," the girl backs away and sits on the couch.

The stranger examines every inch of you. You close your eyes. You are really tired.

"Fuck," the stranger finds the bite on your belly.

"What?" the girl sits up.

"Look at this," the stranger holds you up in an awkward way. You struggle. You just want to be left alone. When you open your eyes, the world is darkening. The girl comes over.

"Oh god, Holden. Were you bit? Did something bite you?"

"Were you going to *keep* this from me?!" the stranger yells at the girl.

"It's just — it's just a scratch," the girl protests. "He got snagged by a branch or something."

"You were gonna let us all die?! Really?! For your fucking *cat?*"

You try to get away from the stranger but she holds you with an iron grip. You hate the yelling. Back home, at the house, whenever there was yelling you would run, find a quiet place, under a bed maybe. But you can't seem to get away here.

You close your eyes and lose consciousness.

A moment later you're outside. The stranger has you by the scruff of your neck with one hand, and holds the shotgun in the other.

Behind her, the girl is crying.

"Stop it! Don't!"

"Julie, I gotta do it! Or eventually we'll *all* get infected. And then what? Huh? Then it's all over."

The stranger steps off the porch and onto the grassy embankment.

She drops you onto the ground and cracks open the shotgun. She reaches into her pocket and loads it.

Despite all the screaming, however, you are now very calm. You have this sense that you are exactly where you are meant to be. This area, at this time,

120

with these people. In the woods, you sense others like yourself. The woods are teeming with others. You are not alone. A thousand sparking intelligences. They trust you to do what you need to do. For the good of all.

Through the sound of the girl sobbing you make a decision.

Do you run? If so, take off to page 169.

If you stay put, turn to page 123.

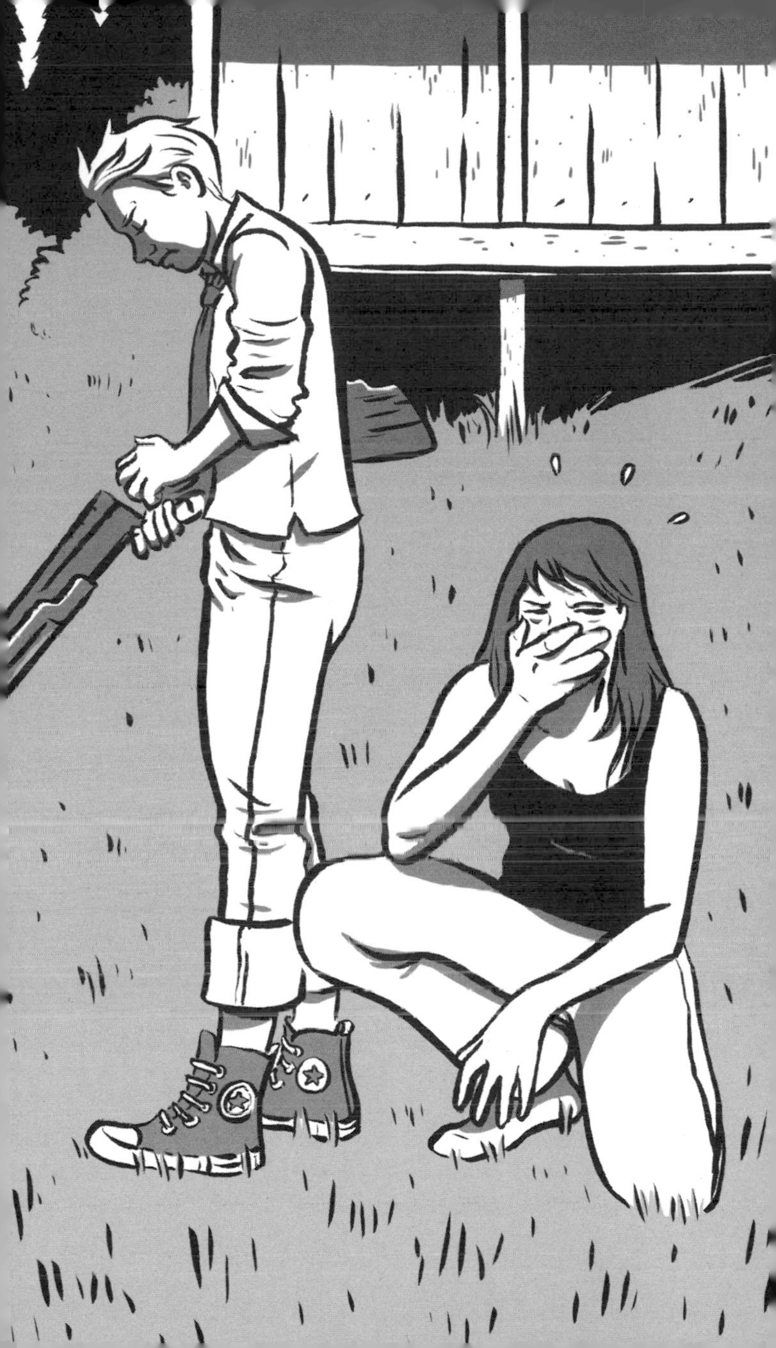

122

Holding the silver fish still with a paw, you sink your teeth into its soft side. As it struggles in your mouth, you bite tighter. Its insides squish.

But wait. It doesn't taste right.

You've had a bunch of fish in your life, raw and processed and otherwise but you don't like this. You spit the fish out. Torn, mangled, it continues to writhe on the rocks.

You try to cough up the rest of whatever you have left in your mouth. You move over to the water, lap some up, try to wash it out.

Kaff! Kaff!

You look over at the fish. Why didn't it die?

It shoud be dead.

You go back over to it. Look down at it.

With a sudden jacknifing movement, the fish nips at your belly!

You jump back.

A small sharp pain where the fish bit.

This is getting worse.

You leave the fish alone.

You need to get back.

Head back to the cabin on page 118.

You sit on the grass staring at the stranger.

The other intelligences tell you they see you and hear you and know what you know and they appreciate you and you are loved and that they are on their way.

The stranger raises the shotgun.

"I'm sorry, Jules," she says.

Sobbing, the girl stands beside the stranger. But then pushes the barrel aside as it fires! The noise is deafening.

The stranger looks sharply at the girl.

"What the hell?!"

The girl runs over to you and lifts you up and hurries you to the woods.

"Julie!" the stranger calls to her. "Let him go!"

The girl stops at the trees and drops you.

"Run, Holden. Get out of here!" She pushes at you with her hands. "Run!"

A rush of warmth from the intelligences, a surge of energy.

They trust you and love you.

Now is your chance to spread the intelligence's warmth. If you choose to listen to the voices in your head and heart, turn to page 124.

If you keep running into the woods, turn to page 169.

You look back at the girl.

"Go!" Tears spill from her eyes, dropping like rain.

The stranger jogs up behind her.

"Jules, he's still dangerous!" she warns.

The girl's hands are outstretched, urging you away. You see the pale green veins underneath her palm. You can smell the blood rushing through them. In one swift movement you are on them, biting into them.

The girl screams, pushes you away.

It tastes good. The intelligences rejoice.

"Fuck! Fuck!" the stranger runs over, jams the end of the shotgun into your face and fires!

Your jaws lose all strength. The force of the blast tosses you into the trees. Your limbs twitch uncontrollably.

From where you are laying, you see the girl holding her hand. It's bleeding freely.

"Oh no, oh no," she says, over and over, like a prayer.

When the stranger catches her breath, she pauses for a moment, a sticken look on her face. Then, she reluctantly lifts the gun to the girl's face.

Slow realization, like an uncertain cloudy day that resolves into a summer storm, crosses the girl's features.

"Do what you got to do," the girl says. Then screams, "Do it!"

Now water spills from the stranger's eyes.

Your body is dying. Darkness is overtaking you. The intelligences can only offer you so much strength from so far away.

The stranger puts the gun down.

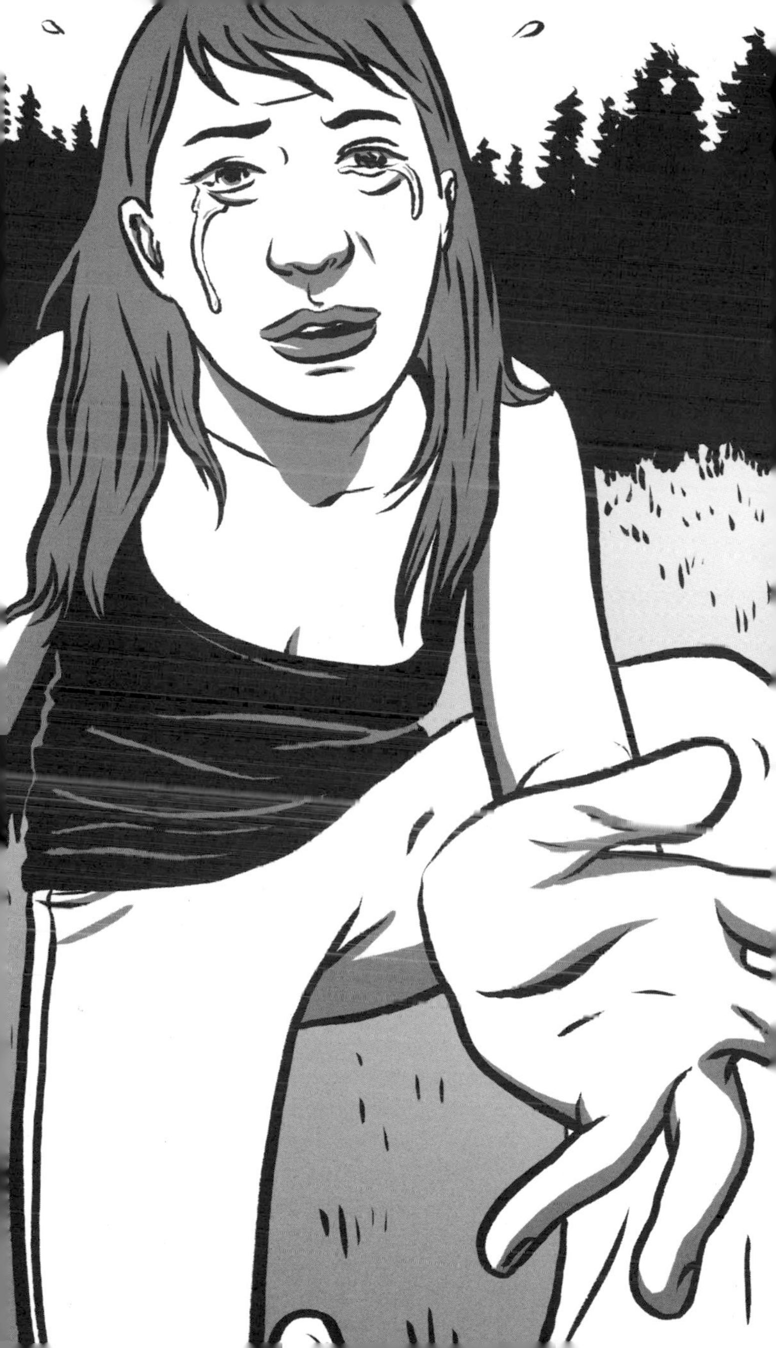

126

"I can't," she says. "I can't."
"What are we going to do?" the girl asks.
Your body dies.

THE END

You leave the fish alone for now. It smells sort of strange. Maybe the voices ahead have a treat or something for you.

You step lightly along the river's edge, moist soil dotted with smooth rocks, and make your way around the bend.

You smell the campfire before you see it. Two men, one short and one tall, stand around it, a large red tent behind them. Around the site various bags litter the ground. Half in and half out of the river, a canoe sits. The two men are talking, and at their feet is a small white bucket that intermittently makes a little slapping noise. Something is in the bucket.

"He says its just food poisoning," the tall one says.

"We don't know that for sure," the short one points at the bucket. "Maybe that fish has got like, leprosy or something. It should be dead. It's been out of the water an hour. It should be fucking *dead*. Something's weird, Lou."

"No, no. That's not necessarily the case. I read this story once about a goldfish that survived seven hours outside the bowl."

"You're missing the point. We need to take him back to the city."

"He's sleeping it off."

"He's sick, man. Eric's sick. What if it's something serious?"

"We've been planning this trip for months! You want to go back now? *You* take him!"

"Fuck!" The short man kicks a rock in exasperation. Then, after a moment, "How far is the car?"

"You're serious?"

"I'll take him."

"God!"

128

"At least we need to get him out of this tent! I think I saw some cabins around here. Maybe we can get him a bed. Get him inside someplace."

The bucket thumps.

"Should we cook it?" the tall one says.

"I'm not eating *that* — diseased fucking fish."

Do you emerge from hiding and show yourself?
Maybe the men have something to
eat or drink on page 139.

If you decide instead to backtrack to the cabin,
turn to 161.

Climbing the interlaced wire, you gain enough purchase to get close to the latch.

The birds stir. You can smell their fear.

Suddenly, more than anything, you want inside the coop.

You bat at the latch. The one at home you have to reach by jumping, but sometimes you can get it just by standing on the edge of the tub. This one is both easier and more difficult.

You push at the hook — then, just like that, it opens.

One large section of the coop wall is hinged into a door, and that swings open slightly as you climb down.

The birds are going crazy. They know what's up.

Your girlfriend is making all these cute little anticipatory noises. You have only heard these sounds from her when there is wet food and it is being held just out of reach by her owner.

When you are mostly back on the ground, you pull open the door with one paw and your girlfriend immediately dives in.

You quickly follow.

The coop is a rampage of panicked fluttering and fear. Some of the birds shit themselves in the chaos.

Several of the birds have already escaped, but plenty remain. Some seem so shocked by your intrusion, they don't know what to do. They simply beat their wings and fly in circles, trying not to look at you.

You claw at everything indescriminately at the beginning, just for fun. You love the feeling of holding a tiny thing down and feeling it struggle against you. And then the reward of tasting it.

Your girlfriend has one pretty grey pigeon in her

130

grasp. Now she has its head in her mouth. Its wings protest, but she doesn't care. You have never seen her so beautiful, so happily frantic. A few blood drops stain its feathers.

More birds escape — you claw at their fleeing bodies — but they don't go far. Many of them perch close by on the edges of the roof, watching, a fearful audience.

When you pause to catch your breath, you have one dead bird on the floor in front of you, and a couple of wounded clinging to the high branches of the coop. Your girlfriend is idly gnawing on her bird. You watch her eyes glisten.

Suddenly, all the birds on the roof fly off and the ones in the coop with you go quiet.

What's going on?

You glance out at the roof. The tomcat has appeared by the fire escape!

He glares at you.

If you try to flee, jump out of the coop and run on page 147.

If instead you decide that staying in the coop is smarter, turn to 132.

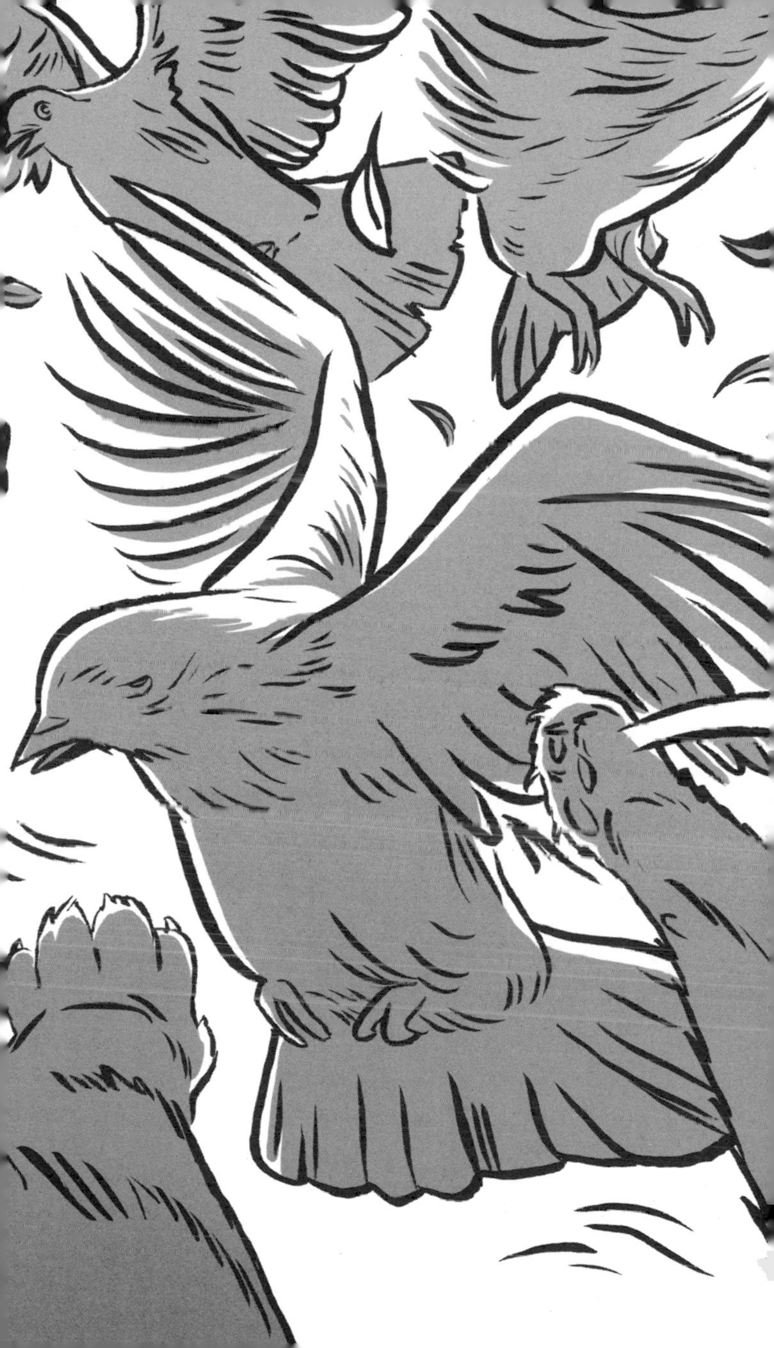

The tomcat starts toward you.

Instinctively you grab the coop door — hold it closed with your claws.

His smooth stalk turns into a gallop. The tom is ferociously fast.

When he gets a few feet from the coop he launches himself into the air! Bashes into the cage. He falls to the ground and withdraws, leaping and bashing again!

Your girlfriend, who moments ago was having the time of her life, has now completely forgotten the bird she was killing. It lays on the ground waving one wing intermittently.

You watch the tom, fascinated. Every time he falls back onto the ground, he seems to have difficulty getting up again. As if he has to pop his bones back into place.

Finally, he stops, glaring at you. You can't believe any cat has eyes that red.

Then he wails — the ululating noise shattering the quiet.

It is long and persistent — unearthly.

Something hits the coop and falls to the ground!

You stare. It's a bird. It twitches.

Another bird hits the coop!

And another!

They're not pigeons. They're smaller.

Where are all these birds coming from?

Like gigantic hailstones, more and more birds slam into the coop, punctuating the tom's constant cry.

Your girlfriend comes over to you, presses herself against you.

You press back, grateful for her company.

This whole thing is terrifying. Maybe staying was a mistake.

Now a huge dog lopes up from the fire escape, its nails clicking on the metal roof lip.

The tom doesn't acknowledge it, but somehow you know it knows it's there.

The dog begins its run over.

Is it going to slam into the coop too?

Suddenly, the dog slows. One more bird his the coop, then the deluge stops. You survey the mass of dark twitching birds on the ground around you. The tomcat closes its eyes, pauses for a moment, then opens them again. He turns. Something else has its attention, but you can't tell what it is.

The dog goes back to the fire escape and descends. The tomcat follows.

You're not going to question this, but it's puzzling.

You and your girlfriend stand there, motionless, as everything calms down.

Then she's pushing at the coop door. You uncouple your claws from the wire and it opens. The both of you step out onto the roof.

You hear something — something from the street below.

The both of you hop up to the roof's metal edge and look down.

A single grey car sits in the street, waves of infected humans and animals surrounding it. The people inside don't move, as if they are afraid any sudden movement will incite attention.

You watch as a dark shape threads its way through the crowd then jumps up onto the front of the car. It's the tomcat!

134

He wails, and from out of the sky tiny birds plummet into the windshield of the car.

One or two don't do anything, but eventually a crack appears as more and more spiral down.

You need to leave while you can.

From your vantage point, you can see that the alley is quite abandoned — all the action localized in the street. It's time to move. You turn around and your girlfriend is already by the fire escape.

The both of you head down the fire escape and make your way to quieter streets on page 65.

"He won't do it," the woman says.

"That's weird," the man replies. "Why not? Maybe there's something different about this subject."

"A trace of his former self?"

"Maybe it's the fact that it's a cat. Maybe the infection affects certain animals differently."

Listening to them, you kind of understand them. You know what they're saying. It's kind of crazy. That you even understand enough to know that this is kind of crazy is kind of crazy. What's going on?

Maybe it's your connection to the collective. You are sharing information, knowledge, souls. It makes sense that just as they can see what you see, you can hear and understand the way humans can other humans.

You want to talk to these two. You want to tell them that love is coming for them and they will not be able to escape it. That love will jump on them and cover them with kisses until they fall on the floor with gratitude and their blood spills out like a palpable happiness.

You try to get your mouth muscles to tell them, but only a gurgle comes out.

The man looks at you. "Uh oh," he says. "Is he gonna barf?"

"I *have* a cat," the woman replies. "When they hack up a furball it's not like that."

"Aurugh," you say.

"Hmm. There's something wrong with this one. How many more infected cats do we have?"

"Two more. The teams also have a dog and a few twitching birds."

"Birds? How'd they catch those?"

"They don't fly too good."

"Well, if we have more, let's vivisect this one," the woman says. "See what his brain looks like."

The man nods and switches off his camera. The red light blinks off.

The woman and man leave and then three larger men in special suits come in. They grab you and put you in another cage. You try to bite one of them, but you clamp down on a fabric made of tiny steel links.

This cage is dark. It's a black box with a few holes. Dim light streams in. You put your eye to a hole, but can only see passing walls.

Finally the ride is over and the men remove you from the cage. Gloved hands grab your limbs. You struggle but are unable to do anything. They place you on a board belly up, then they stretch out your arms and legs and zip-tie them down. It's cold.

The woman arrives with a needle in her blue-gloved hands.

"Ready?" she asks.

"Recording now," the man says. You turn your head and see him. The red light is back on.

"Let's see how much anesthesia he can take. We'll start with a small dose and work our way up."

The next two hours are awful.

Repeated needles make you sleepy. And then, when you are drowsy but not out, they start cutting your body. The worst is that you are awake for all this.

"Surprisingly little blood," the woman says, scalpel in hand. She wears a mask but you know it's her.

"Well, he's a zombie."

"I know. But you know zombie movies. Aren't those gore fests?"

"The blood's usually from other people."

Later, after they've removed most of your skin,

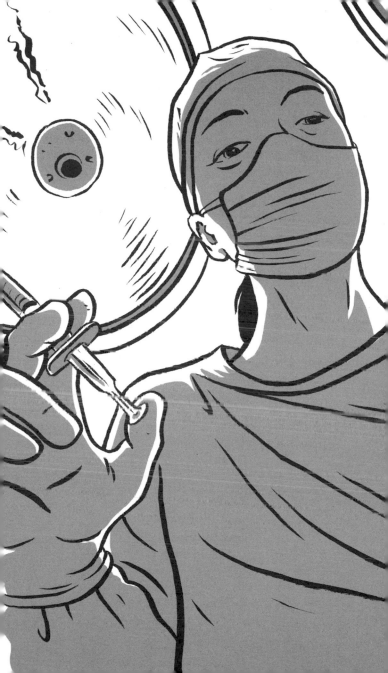

and cut your hind legs off the woman turns you around, restrains you face down at your wrists and tail.

"Going to cut the central nervous system now. Finally we'll know if we need to aim for the brain or the spine."

You feel a pressure on your neck. Then, nothing.

The woman appears in your vision. She moves to the right. You follow her with your eyes.

"Brain," she says. "Definitely brain."

"Well, let's test that hypothesis then." the man replies cooly.

The woman goes over to a tray and lifts a small tool with a spinning circle at the end. She sets it whirring then moves over to you.

You feel a pressure on the top of your head before everything goes dark.

Immediately the collective is there to soothe and collect you.

Our love is forever, they tell you.

There is no more pain, only love.

THE END

"Hey," the tall man nods over at you. "Look."

"What?" The short man turns, sees you. "It's a cat. What's a cat doin' out here?"

The tall man bends down, "Hey kitty. C'mere."

You make your way over to him. Smells of cooking emanate from a pile of dishes set beside a tree stump. From inside the tent, a cough.

"I have an idea," the tall man says to his friend. "Let's get the fish to bite the cat. See what happens."

"What do you think will happen?" the short one says sharply. "We'll have a sick *cat*, too!"

"Maybe. Maybe not. We need to isolate the cause. Is this something that *we* could get? Or is it really just food poisoning?"

The short man nods. "How do we do this?"

The tall man makes cooing noises and beckons to you. You go over to him and he picks you up.

"Hey kitty," he smiles. You begin to purr. You know they have food. Maybe they'll give you some.

The short man gets the bucket. A regular thump thump, like a heartbeat comes from something inside.

"What's wrong?" the man holding you asks.

"I don't wanna touch it."

"Get the skinning gloves."

The short man goes to a bag and pulls out a pair of black rubber gloves. He slips them on, then comes over with the bucket.

Curious, you try to get a glimpse. The short man reaches into the bucket.

"Hold still, you little shit," he murmurs to himself. When his arm comes out, he is holding a fish! They're giving you a fish!

This is awesome.

140

The tall man's arms tense as the fish comes near. "Hold him!"

Wait. Why is the man so tense? The fish looks weird. Looks like the fish you saw at the river. Smells wrong. Looks wrong. Everything's wrong. You squirm, your arms pushing against the tall man.

"I said hold him *still!*"

"Shit! He's getting loose!"

You jump to the ground. You need to run. But to where? A quick look around gives you two options.

If you run to the river, turn to page 153.

Or if you think you can find a hiding spot in the red tent, retreat there on page 168.

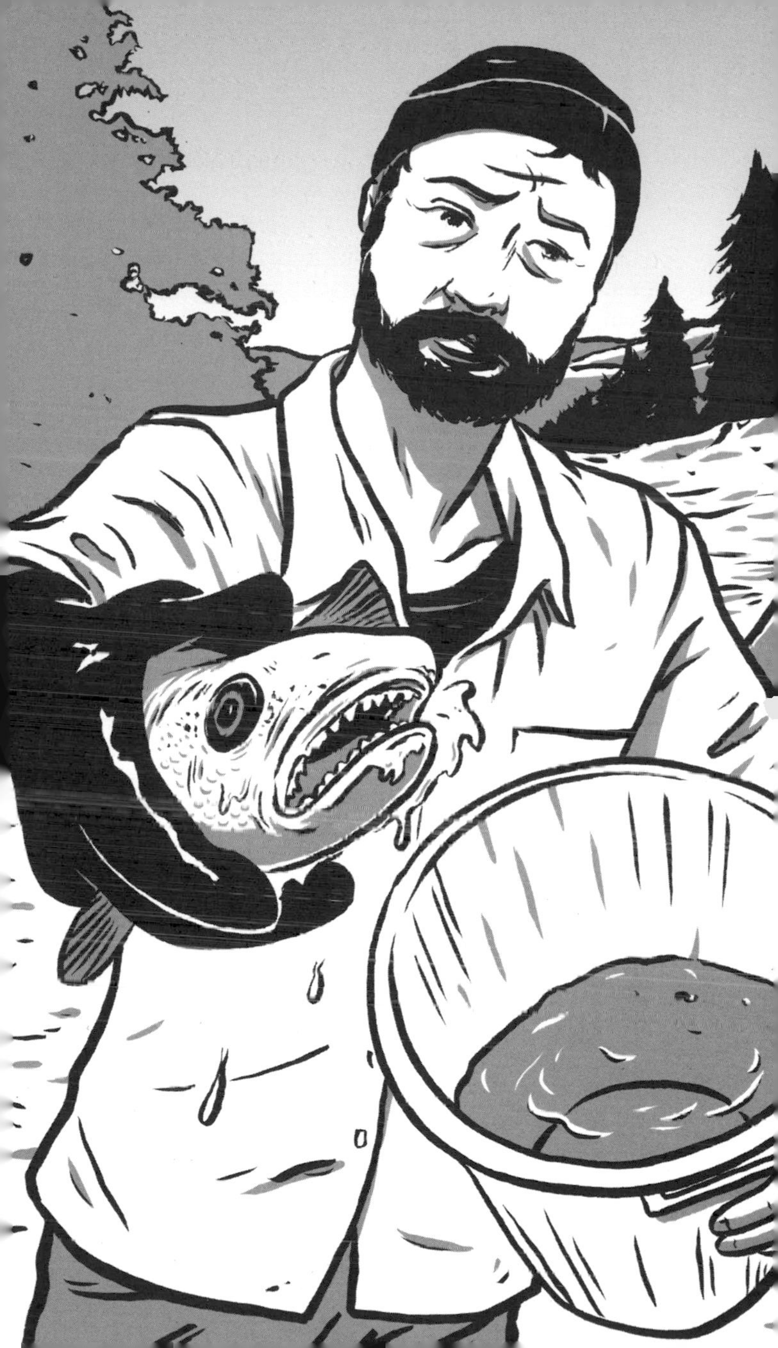

Suddenly the birds go nuts.

They are flapping and crying and flying with nowhere to go.

You look over at your girlfriend, but she is looking at you. Neither of you did anything.

Then your girlfriend looks over your shoulder. She stiffens, and her pupils dilate like eclipsing suns.

You turn around.

It's the tomcat! He stands at the edge of the roof. He followed you.

He opens his mouth and lets out a monstrous wail. You can see every single one of his teeth.

Now he jumps down to the gravelled roof and runs toward you!

You and your girlfriend flee.

The only other things on this roof are a couple of large white metal boxes, but they won't give you much cover.

You jump up onto the edge of the roof, a grey metal surface and run along that.

Terrifyingly, the world drops down to the street on your right.

You see the tomcat.

He runs unhesitatingly towards you, closing in.

He's going to jump!

Abruptly, you stop and roll down onto the roof while he is in mid-air.

Open mouth dripping saliva, as if to chomp you, the tomcat misses you and disappears off the side!

You begin to hear a wail, but it is cut short.

Out of breath, you and your girlfriend look over the edge.

The tomcat lies unmoving on the ground below.

The two of you don't stop to see if his wails at-

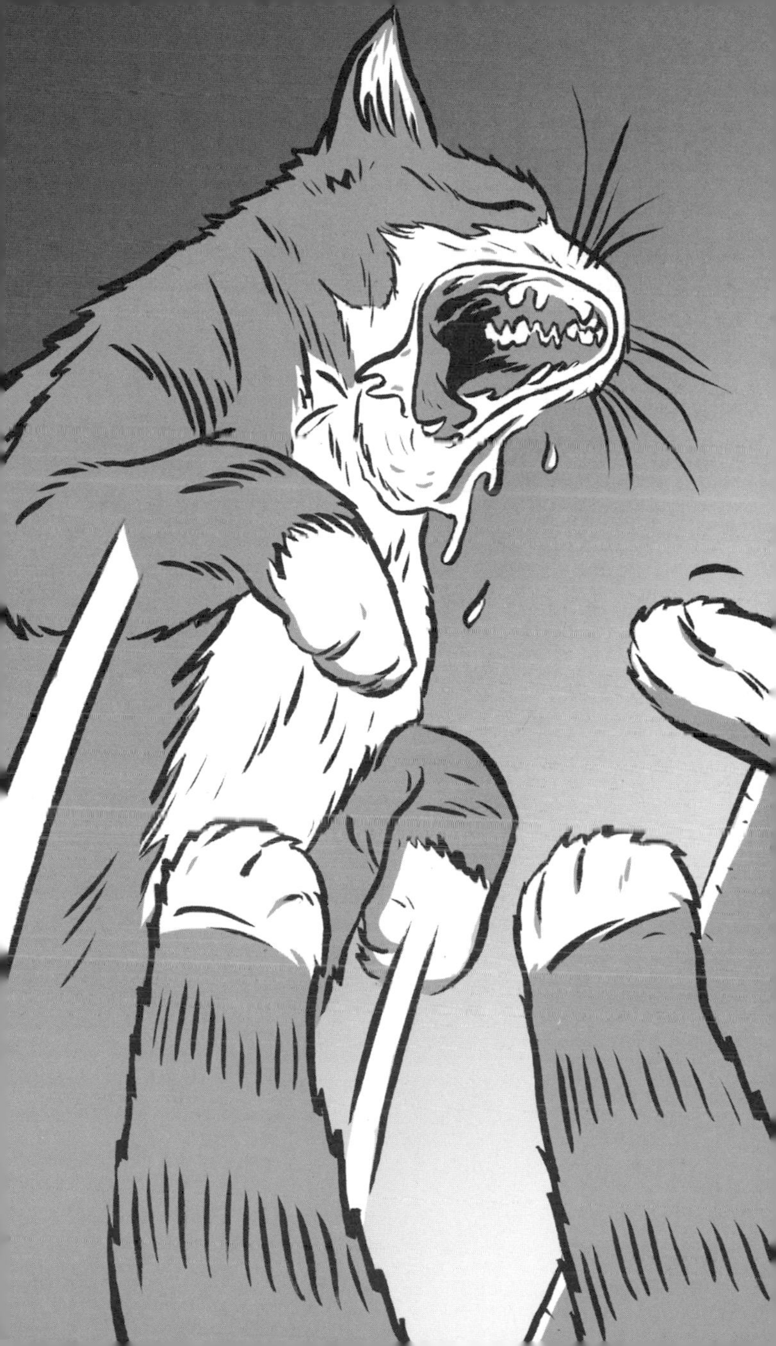

tracted any of the infected. You go back down the fire escape and run along the streets, close to the walls and parked cars, heading for any street that seems quieter than this one.

Turn to page 65.

You stand in the shadow of the tree. You can smell the faint trace of her scent, but no sight of her.

Then you hear a noise from above.

You look up.

Is your girlfriend back up in the tree? Why?

Maybe the noise from the men in the trucks scared her back there.

You mewl up at her.

Then, a dark silhouette falls from a branch, growing large.

Too fast for you to move out of the way!

Your girlfriend lands on you. Her usual scent is strange, perverted.

Her teeth rip your throat out.

In the midst of sudden blood loss, you wonder what happened.

Will you come back as one of them?

That's a lot of blood on your chest.

You don't wonder for long.

THE END

You venture out into the street. Immediately the man sees you. He swings his rifle at you.

"Cat!" he says.

Your girlfriend, taking your lead, also comes out. Do they have food for you?

"One of them's got blood on its face!"

"You are clear to engage," a voice crackles from the speaker clipped to the man's clothes.

"Acknowledged," the man says.

When he starts firing, sparks kick up from the road in front of you! Then your girlfriend is jolted, falls, and doesn't move.

You freeze.

What's happening?

You are punched somehow in the shoulder, and then the chest.

You wheel and flop on the ground.

You land at an odd angle so one ear is folded uncomfortably behind your head but you find that you are unable to move to relieve it.

You look over at your girlfriend. Her eyes are dead as they stare at you.

This is the last thing you ever see.

THE END

You and your girlfriend quickly leave the coop. The tom doesn't move from his spot near the fire escape. He knows that that's the only way down.

You survey the roof — assessing your options.

The tom's piercing wail shatters your concentration. You stare at him. What kind of noise is that? It's awful.

A dark bird shakily swoops down.

Almost too late you realize two things: that it's a crow, and it's aimed at you!

You bat at it with your paw, knocking it to the ground.

You look up. More black dots appear overhead.

Your girlfriend seems to understand quicker than you do — she takes off at a run. You follow.

In your wake, you hear the sound of birds smacking gravel.

For a second, you take shelter behind one of the large white metal boxes that dots the rooftop. Birds colliding into that make a different noise. You understand that you can't stay here. Already high above the birds are swinging around to come down at you from a different angle.

Suddenly the wailing stops.

You peek around the corner of the box.

The tomcat is coming for you himself!

Your girlfriend takes off. Where is she going? She jumps up onto the edge of the roof and keeps up her sprint. You do the same though it is terrifying. Right beside you is a huge drop to the street.

You look ahead past her.

Now you understand.

There is another building. Its roof is slightly lower than the one you're on. You are separated from it only by a thin alley.

It almost happens in slow motion. Your girlfriend approaches the edge. Her pale body not slowing for a second. She times her gait just right. Her hind paws grasp the very edge and she pushes off!

She is like a bird herself as she leaps across the gap!

You are about to follow when suddenly you lose all courage.

You skid to a stop at the very corner of the roof.

You watch your girlfriend land perfectly on the other side, somersaulting onto the dark tar roof. She scrambles to her feet and then looks back at you.

You look away.

You don't know if you can do this.

You have failed jumps before in spectacularly embarassing ways.

Once, back home, you tried to jump from the stove to the kitchen table. You miscalculated on the take-off and smacked your face into the floor. You didn't try any risky jumps for days after.

Your girlfriend meows at you, expectantly.

You feel a slight vibration on the metal ledge. Oh no. You look back. The tom has jumped up onto the roof ledge as well.

Well that's decided it.

Going against all your instincts, you move along the ledge towards the tom. All you want to do is get *away* from him, but you understand you need room to work up some speed. When you think it's enough, you turn.

The tomcat speeds up behind you.

You gallop to the ledge. You leap!

In mid-air you look over at your girlfriend. Her

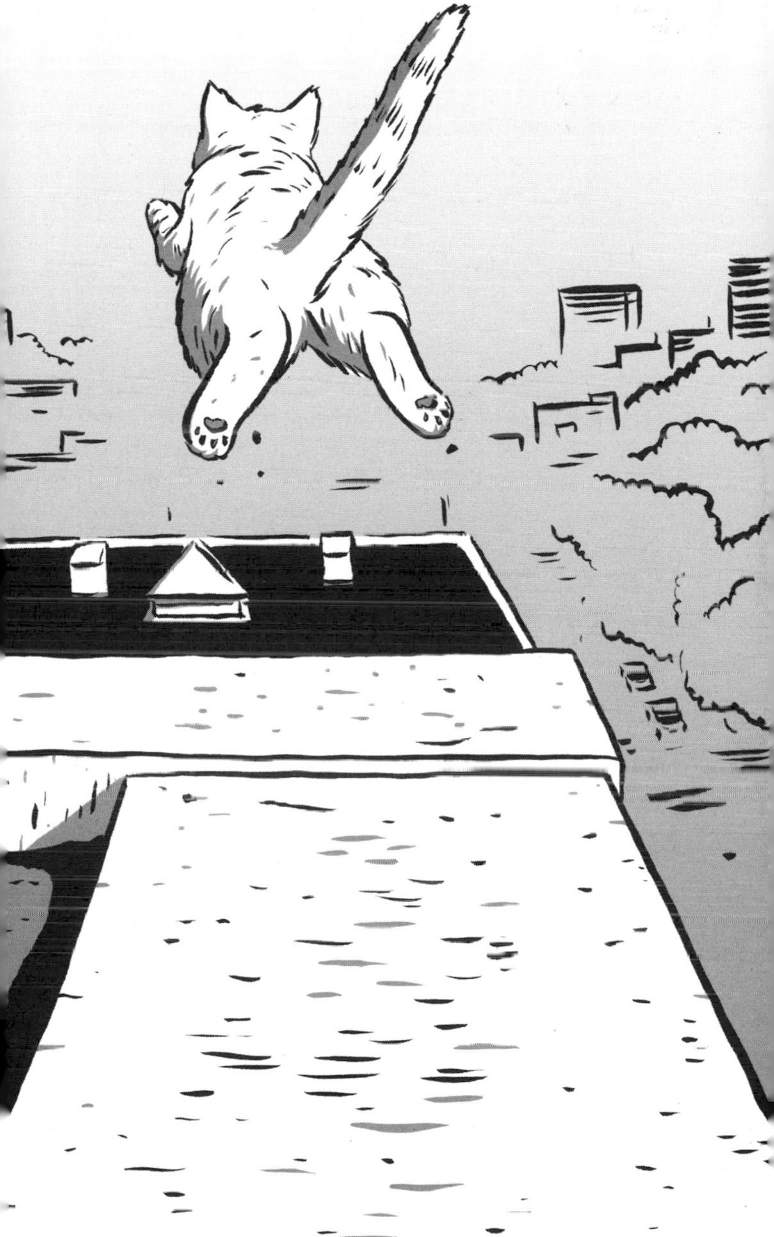

eyes full of fear and hope for you.

You hope you have pushed off hard enough.

You haven't.

As you begin your descent you realize your miscalculation.

Your forepaws slam into the roof edge, and the full weight of your body slides down the side of the wall. You scramble, claws trying to find purchase but slipping. You are slipping!

Suddenly your girlfriend appears at the edge, reaching for you!

She sinks her claws into your arm. With your other arm you snag a brick.

Your hindlegs scrabble for something — *anything* — and then they have it! Some kind of wire, fastened to the wall below you. You push off of that, and with your girlfriend's help, you manage to haul yourself over the top.

You have hardly had time to catch your breath when your girlfriend gives off a startled cry.

You turn to look.

The tom, red eyes blazing, is in mid-leap.

Somehow the jump is like nothing to him.

With a howl your girlfriend braces herself, then with both paws *pushes* the tom in his face before he lands!

Just like you, his body hits the wall and he begins to fall. He scrambles to hang on.

The two of you watch him struggle.

Finally he is hanging on by a claw.

"Heh, heh," he pants. Then the claw tears and he falls!

On the way down his unearthly wail starts again, but quickly halts when he hits the ground.

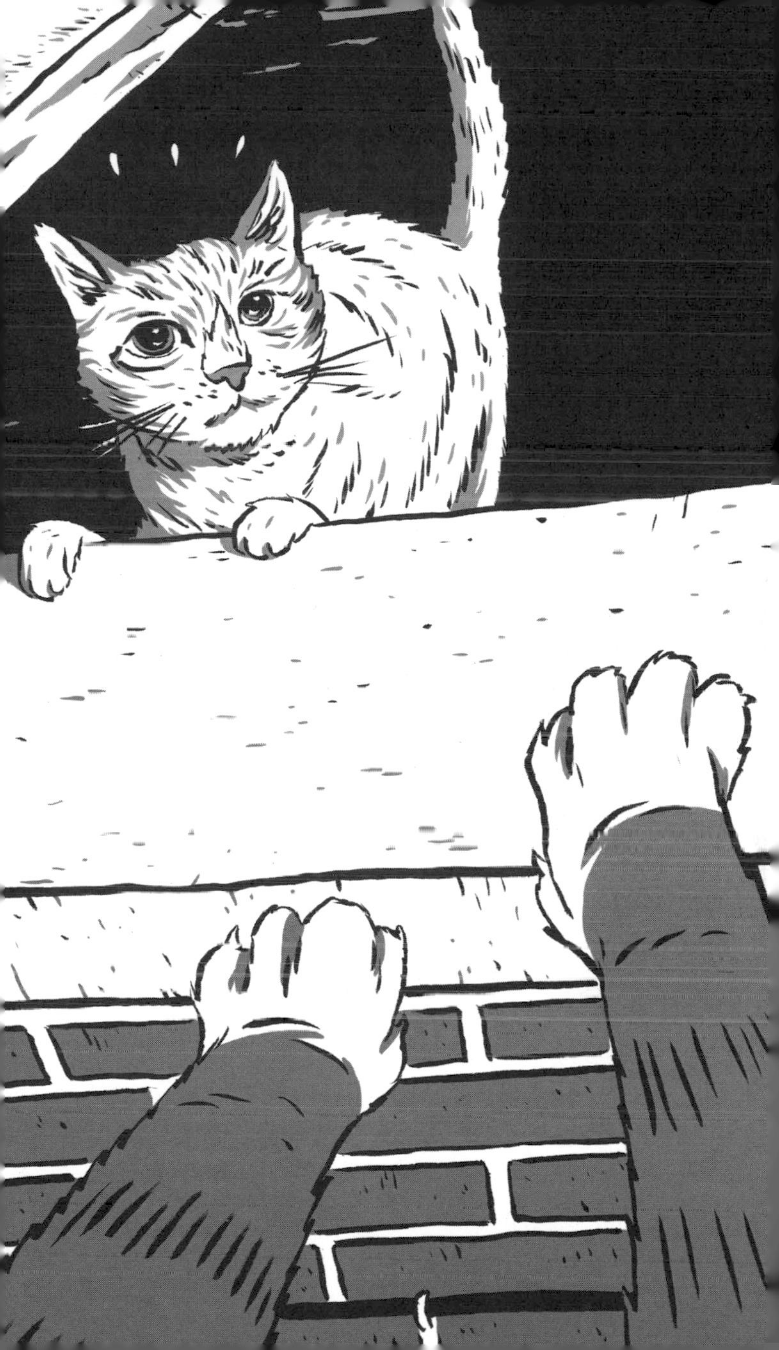

152

You and your girlfriend take a few moments to catch your breath before dropping down to a fire escape and making your way down to the street.

That was insane.

As the two of you huddle beside a pungent garbage can, a large green truck rumbles along the street, then stops. A man in clothes the same colour as the truck sits on top, looking around.

Your stomach grumbles and you wonder if he might have some food.

It's been a long day so far. You could do with something to eat.

If you show yourself in the hopes of getting food, turn to page 146.

If you decide it might be better to hide, turn to 94.

You race to the river. You aren't entirely sure what's wrong, but listening to your gut has kept you alive this long, and you aren't about to start questioning it.

"Lou, chase him!"

You hear long strides displacing tiny, clattering rocks.

"Kitty! It's okay! Come back!" the man yells.

The ground gets damp below your feet. In front of you is a boat, half in the water, which you jump into. You clamber over to the far end.

The tall man slows, crouches, bends low. A smile comes to his face.

"Hey," he whispers. He offers his hand, like he's friendly. But he's not. "Where are you going now? Huh? You're cornered. You aren't going *anywhere*."

You look at him, then at the water, then back at him.

The man steps gingerly into the boat. It shifts underneath you. The end you're at begins to drift out into the current. You don't like this at all.

"C'mere," he brings his other foot into the boat.

You decide to run underneath him, and hopefully get back onto shore. But as you make your move, the man grabs your tail!

But then —

With a sickening shake, the man loses his balance and overturns the boat! You try to leap for shore but you end up in the water!

Ugh! Water. You do your best to swim, but you don't have much experience, and the whole thing is so awful you are fighting your own misery just to stay afloat.

You need to get away. You decide to swim to the

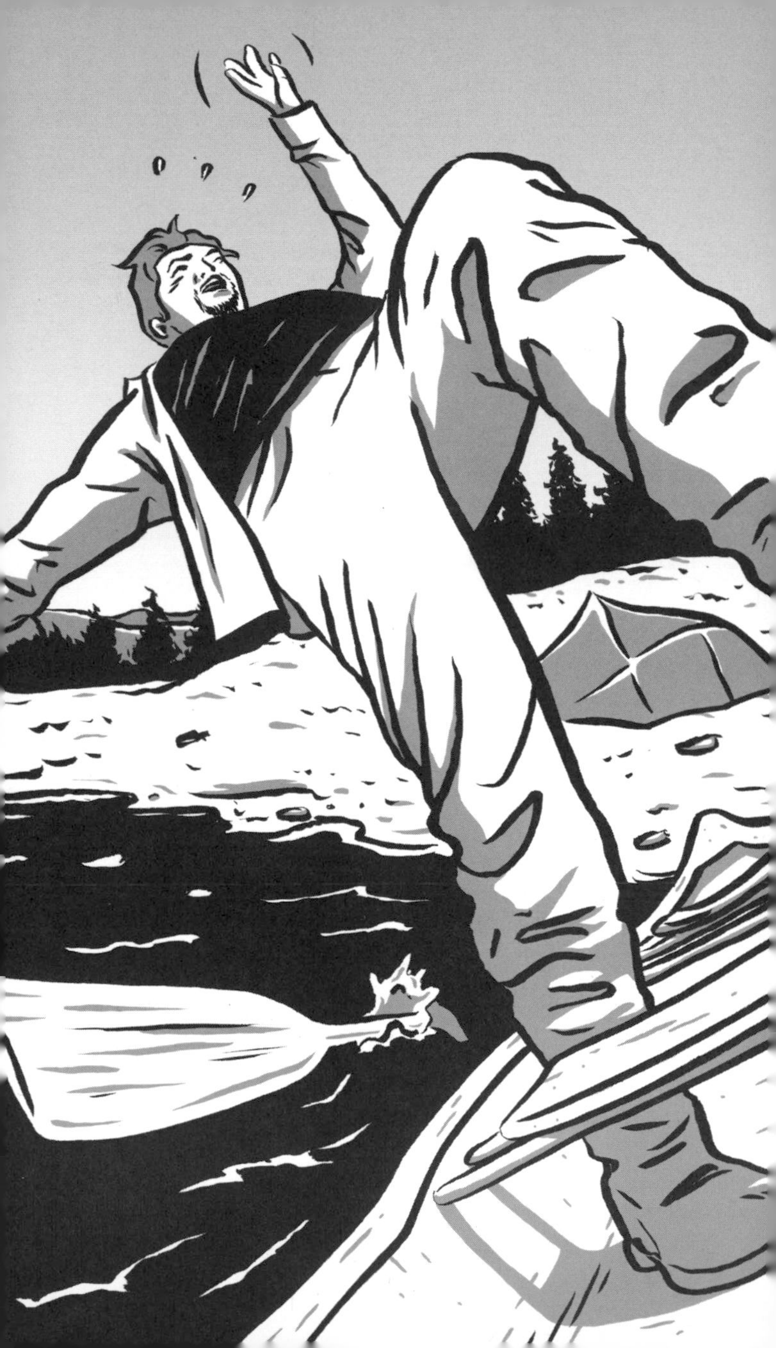

other side. Fighting the current, you manage to get most of the way there, when you hear a yell from shore.

By the tent, the short man is waving his arm. The tiny fish is biting down on his wrist, the exposed flesh between glove and shirt.

"Ahhh!" he screams. "It won't let go!"

The tall man sputters up from the river, sloshing onto shore.

"Kev, I'm coming!"

Dripping mightily, the man runs to help his friend remove the fish.

Meanwhile, you finally crawl up onto the rocks on the other side.

Chilled, with cold water sluicing down your slick fur, you move into the woods.

You sneeze, then sneeze again.

Eventually you find a nice bush to hide under. It's dark and that's comforting.

You hear the gentle patter of a slow rain on the leaves overhead. You move your mouth over to the dripping rainwater and lap some up.

Despite your dampness, you are still thirsty.

You can't get warm. But at least the shivering is now less intense. At first it was crazy but now it's thankfully abated.

"Hey, Holden," you hear.

You start.

It's the girl. You look around the bush you're under.

Where is she?

"Hey, Holdy..." she says again.

You come out from underneath the bush and start following the voice.

156

"Holden!" you hear her calling for you like she sometimes does from the backdoor of the house.

You're coming! You start moving through the woods, shivering and stumbling. Where is she?

Then, in the distance, you see her. She waves to you.

You sneeze again, and when you look back up, she's gone. Undaunted, you keep heading in the direction you last saw her.

But you can't find her.

Finally, exhausted, you lie down in the crotch of a tree and look up at its tall dark trunk and leafy branches.

"Holden," you hear. Then she's there.

You're in her lap. The girl looks down at you, holding you in her arms. She's in her pajamas. Rain drizzles steadily down on her and you.

But now the sun has come out, shining through the raindrops, making them sparkle. The girl smiles at you and reaches to stroke your head.

Your shaky breath plumes steadily upwards into her face.

You're glad she found you.

You're home.

THE END

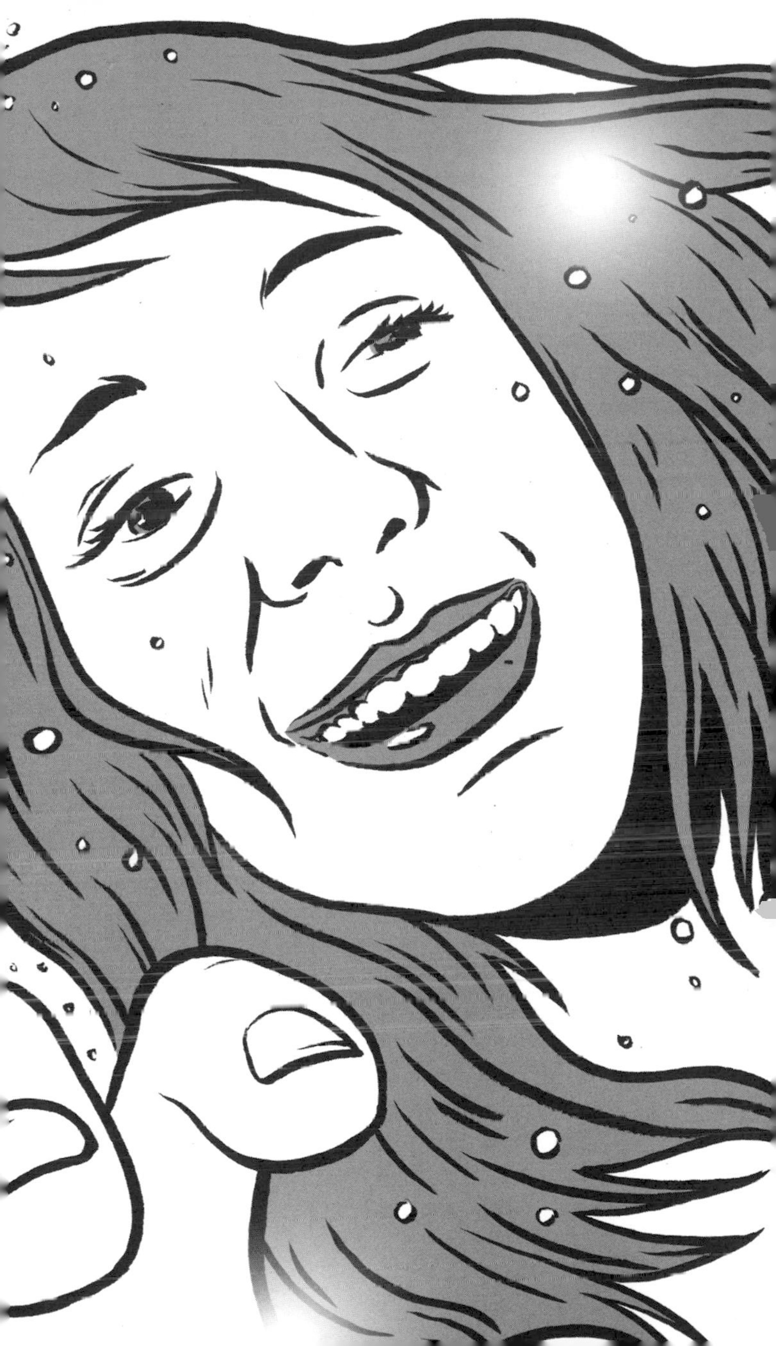

158

You move closer to the girl and she giggles. Then you bite her wrist!

"Aieeeeeee!" the girl screams. She punches at you. You gnash at her flesh, and blood spills from her wrist.

Everyone who is eating turns to see what the commotion is all about. A woman comes running. "Taylor! What's the matter? What's the matter, honey?"

Releasing the girl, you take off. Hopefully you won't have to come back. Hopefully the girl will spread the love amongst the others. You'll see. Soon you'll be able to sense her.

You must find others to safely spread your love to.

You run to page 85.

The woman comes back inside and shuts the front door, shaken.

"Don't shoot what?" she asks the girls. "What *was* that?"

The younger girl comes over to you and picks you up.

"They're ours."

"Katie," the woman speaks through gritted teeth. "Drop that cat. Right now."

"But — "

"Drop it!"

The girl drops you abruptly, and you walk over to the window. There is a little display of items there and you jump up onto it to get a better look outside. Where is your girlfriend? You peer through the glass at the parking lot outside. Ringing the parking lot is a strip of lawn, and a few trees grow. In the shadow of a tree you think you see a shape that might be your girlfriend but you are not sure.

"What are you doing Mom?"

You turn to see the woman pointing the gun at you.

"Don't!" the two girls are holding their mother.

"It might be sick," the woman says. "You don't know. You don't understand."

"Please Mom!" the little girl is crying.

You look around. This is weird. You don't like all this attention. There's too much tension in her expression. You need to get away.

A high sharp scream and then an even louder *bang*.

Your heart explodes and the window behind you shatters!

You fall onto your back.

160

It's hard to breathe. You can't breathe.

You can't hear either. The enormous noise has left your hearing ringing.

You see the two girls fall onto their knees. The woman stands, shocked expression on her face.

You turn your head and look out the window.

Cool night air caresses your fur.

You think you see your girlfriend step out of the shadow of the trees and into the light of the streetlamp, but it dissolves into a throbbing splash of incohate luminescence, pulsating into darkness.

THE END

You decide to head back to the cabin. You are not sure you trust these men. They're keyed-up about something and tense people are usually not very generous with treats.

As you backtrack along the river you look for the silver fish but it's not there anymore. It must have flipped itself back into the water. Oh well.

Wait. Where was the cabin? You look around. The gusts off the hills are quite strong, and have blown your scent away. You smell around but none of your scent remains, and none of the woods look familiar.

But then one tree looks familiar.

Did you pass that? You move over to it.

Maybe.

You stride into the woods, deciding it's the way.

But it's not the way. After a long while you realize you are lost.

You wander the woods. Occasionally you mewl.

Can they hear you? You want the girls to find you.

You let out another long, meandering mewl.

Nothing. Nothing to do but keep walking.

You spend the whole day walking, when, miraculously — the sun almost gone, its faint glow rimming the hilltops — you get back to the cabin.

It's very quiet. You have barely the strength to scratch at the cabin door.

You hear movement inside.

The girl opens it, just a little. Not enough for you to get in, however.

"Holden?" she says, tentatively.

You mewl plaintively. Why won't she let you in? You push your head against the opening.

The girl laughs.

"Awright," she opens the door. "C'mon in.

Where've you been?"

You head inside and sniff the air. There's no food anywhere. You go over to the kitchen, but there's no bowl or anything.

You meow at the girl, complaining.

"Oh shit," the girl says. "You're hungry. And we forgot to get any catfood." The girl closes her eyes and rubs her temples. "I'm such a bad mom."

You meow in frustration. Why isn't there any food?! You keep meowing, just because it feels good, because she should *know*.

The girl looks up. "Do you want some water? Are you thirsty?" The girl goes over to the cupboard. Is she getting food? You go over, close to her legs.

The girl gets a bowl and then goes over to the tap. It coughs a little, then water gushes forth. She fills it and then puts it down in front of you. Even though you knew it would be water, you were kind of hoping it would be food. But water's better than nothing, and so you lap it up. It's not great. Very metallic. But you lap it up anyway because you've been out all day and are tired.

The girl strokes your head and then goes to flop down on the couch.

"Fuck! Where is she?" the girl mutters to herself.

You drink up the water, more than you ever have before.

And when you're done, all you want to do is nap. You clean yourself in the most cursory of ways because all you want is to not be awake and lost in a forest anymore.

You fall asleep in the girl's lap on page 165.

You dart towards the door, slipping expertly past the woman's legs, then out between the bars of the gate.

"Don't shoot *what?!* What do you know about those things? Are those *cats?*"

Behind you, the door closes. You can hear the woman's voice, now muffled, yelling at the girls.

You look around.

Where did your girlfriend go?

There are a couple of cars parked quietly next to each other. Could she be there? Ringing the parking lot is a small lawn, with small trees dotting the perimeter. Under the streetlamps, they cast a black, inky shadow. You normally have good night vision, but the lamps kill it. Could she be by the trees?

You meow experimentally, hoping your girlfriend will call back.

A movement from near the tree.

You venture close.

As your eyes adjust, you make out a man. He moves out from underneath the shadows and approaches!

Instinctively you run away, back toward the gate.

But you understand that it's too open and easy to reach through, and offers no real protection. You stand there, unsure.

More figures appear from the shadows! And, to your left, you see more infected emerging from the other side of the cars.

How are they doing this?

Uncannily, they know in a heartbeat when there's a target. They gather like pigeons when a human is handing out breadcrumbs.

Then you see a fast-dashing blur. It's your girl-

164

friend. You're not sure where she was hiding — maybe under the cars — but she runs along the lawn and climbs up the tree!

If you deke around the infected man and up the tree also, go to page 174.

If instead you run under the cars go to page 180.

When you wake up, the girl is tense.

She is staring out the big bay window at the dark woods and the dark night.

Her stress is this tight ball around her belly and you can feel it. You get up and walk to the other side of the couch and curl up there.

After you get up, the girl brings her knees up to her chin, then wraps her arms around her legs.

"Oh god," the girl says. "It's so late. Where is she?" She fiddles with the phone in her hands. It lights up, then goes dark again.

"No fucking service. No fucking service," the girl mutters to herself.

Suddenly, a loud banging at the door!

You jump up and run into the bedroom, hiding under the bed.

"Who is it!?" the girl yells.

"It's me Jules! Let me in!"

It's the stranger.

You creep over to the bedroom door and watch the stranger slip in and shut the cabin door behind her. Quickly, she shuts off all the lights except the one over the sink.

"Grab the poker," she whispers to the girl. The girl goes over to the fireplace and gets a stick.

"What's going on? Where have you been? You scared me to death! Why didn't you use your keys?"

"It's too dark outside! I couldn't see. Anyway, shh! There's a man out there."

"What?!"

"Shh!"

"What if it's your dad?"

"It's not my dad. I know my dad. This isn't — "
Bam! Bam!

166

Someone's pounding on the door. You retreat back underneath the dresser.

"Leave us alone!" the stranger yells.

"Help!" a small voice, male, calls back. "My friends. They're sick!"

The stranger raises her shotgun. "I'm armed! I have a gun and I *will* use it!"

"Oh god! They're here! Let me in!"

"No! Go away!" the stranger says.

Silence. Then the sounds of the man's footsteps on the porch, moving away.

"Is he gone?" the girl whispers.

No. Not moving away. Moving *around*.

You see the man in the big bay window, a dark shape against a dark forest, his head silhouetted against a sprinkling of stars. He moves back and then moves forward, crashing through the glass!

The high jangly sound pierces your ears.

The man falls into a somersault, his momentum carrying him, and sprawls on the floor in front of you.

Scared out of your mind, something primal takes over.

Run from the man on page 201!

Fight the man on page 186!

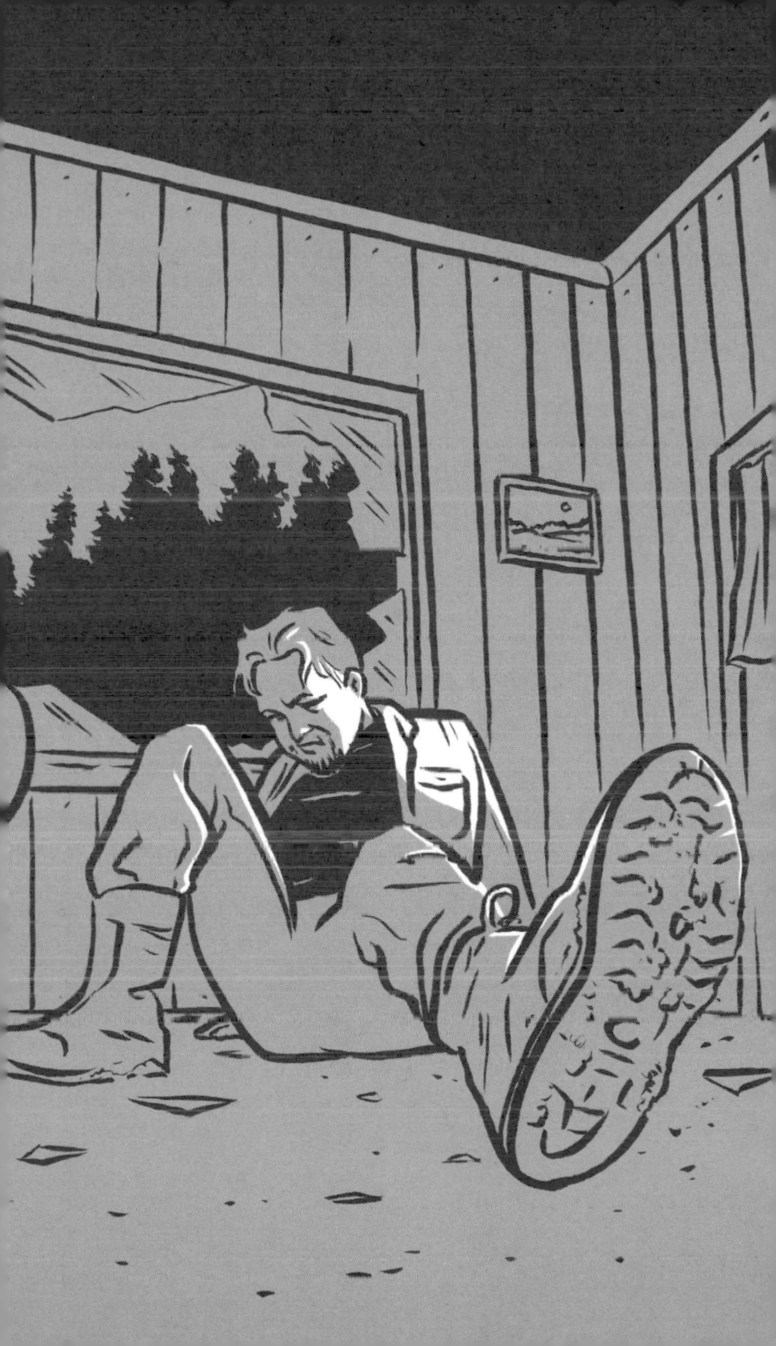

168

You slip through the slit in the tent.

"Shit! He's in there with Eric."

Inside, a man lies on a puffy blanket, eyes closed. You jump onto him, and then over him, against the tent wall.

The sleeping man's eyes ease open, blearily.

The tall and short man widen the slit and poke their faces in. They stare at you. You stare back at them.

Suddenly, the sleeping man grabs you! And with one smooth motion brings you to his face and bites you! You yowl.

"Oh fuck! Eric!" The men disappear from the tent entrance.

The sleeping man drops you and shambles out of the tent.

"Hah, hah," he pants.

On the tent floor you assess yourself. Pain in your belly. The man bit you. A dark shadow rings your vision. Then you pass out.

A moment later, you regain consciousness.

You need to get back to the cabin. The girl can help you. You need help.

As you emerge from the tent you see the short man on his face by the firepit. He's breathing, but he's not moving. Is he sleeping?

The pain in your belly keeps you moving. You backtrack the way you came. You are woozy but you think you can make it.

Get back to the cabin and the girl can help you.

You move slowly but steadily to page 118.

You run into the forest. You don't know where you're going, but that seems less pressing than getting away. When you feel you've gone far enough, you slow, and look back.

"Go! Go!" the girl urges. You keep moving.

But it isn't easy. You are having a hard time catching your breath.

"Hah, hah," you pant. "Hah."

Thick saliva drips down around your lips. You move, but awkwardly. Your limbs feel sleepy, weak.

Footsteps behind you. You turn around. You see the stranger venturing into the woods, searching for you.

"Don't do it!" you hear the girl yell.

"I have to! He'll come back!"

She's close!

An overwhelmingly loud bark from the shotgun. Chips fly off a nearby tree!

Despite your sleepiness, you run under a bush, then behind a tree.

Another report. But this time farther away.

You move furtively into the woods, leaving the girls behind.

Though you are having more trouble navigating the world, at the same time the world is coming alive to you in a way you've never experienced before.

You watch the waving of distant branches of leaves, their tips trembling.

Everything's part of a system. Everything's connected. Just as you are connected. You feel the deeper intelligence in your blood and your brain. As you march forward, you feel that you are part of something larger, something greater.

"Hah, hah," you pant, as you move one paw in

front of the other.

A wave of nausea rolls through you.

A flash vision of the earth, from high above. You've never *been* this high before. You see a dark blob below, moving. It's like a rat without a tail. Then a cloud occludes your vision and you're back on earth.

When you continue, you feel like you know this landscape. You've seen this before from the sky. All this is familiar.

Including the rat.

Who is suddenly in front of you.

But it's not a rat. It's bigger.

The bear spies you from a few car-lengths away. It snorts, then paws the ground. It lets out a huge roar.

You move forward. You want to bite it. You want to love it.

The bear rears up on its back legs, makes itself as big as possible, roars again.

The old you would have run away but now all you want to do is get close.

The bear's nose twitches as it smells you. A moment of confusion. It drops down from its hind legs with a thud, then turns.

You scamper forward and it gallops away. Like it's scared of you.

You can't keep up. Your legs are rickety.

Drawn by an innate sense, eventually you make your way to a clearing.

This is a good place to stop.

You stand in the middle of a field overtaken by wildflowers and weeds, and wait.

Above you, the sky darkens into a deep dark blue. You sit, patient.

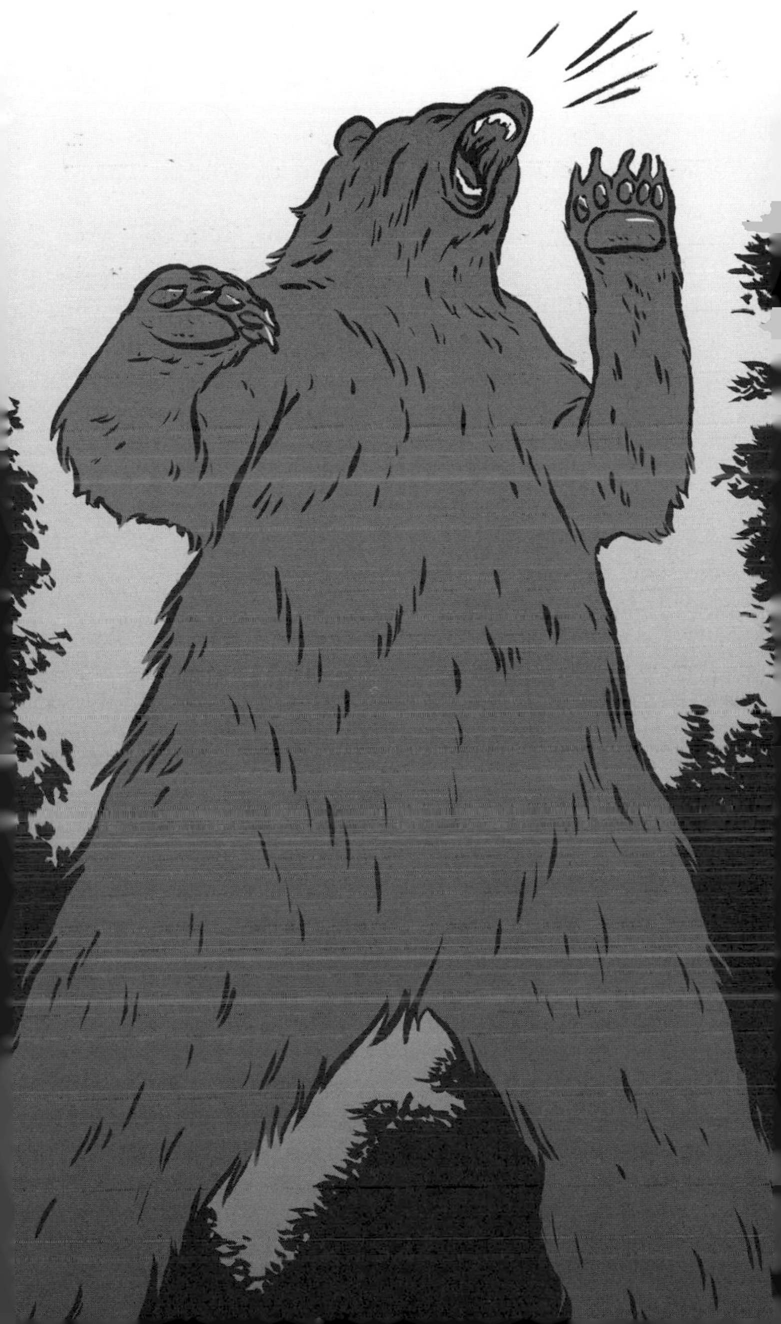

172

The calm, inner intelligent voice talks to you, soothes you, connects you with others. You sense them, out there, approaching.

A squirrel. Then a fox. Coming from all directions, gathering around you. More squirrels. Birds that can only hop. A black-masked raccoon. Hedgehogs. Marmots. Every kind of animal slips out of the surrounding woods to gather around you.

You begin to head back. The creatures follow. A long parade of mammals, silkily streaming through the grass, threading through the woods back toward the cabin.

Yes, there is life there. There is life we need. Life with access to more life.

The torrent of animals moves like a river through the forest. Ahead, you see the light of the cabin.

The animals trust you.

How do we get in?

If you scratch at the door, do so and wait on page 183.

If instead you want the other animals to go first, tell them on page 178.

As your friends are being shot, you run! But when you reach the ground you realize the best place to hide is under the very car you were standing on.

You zip under the car and your heart breaks as each shot is followed by the body of a friend falling to the ground. The bodies drop and pile around the car. Finally it's quiet.

The truck rumbles over and the sharpshooter calls out.

"Ma'am! You in the car! Are you okay?"

Silence.

"Ma'am! Wave if you understand me!"

"Any response?" a voice through his radio asks.

"No. Let's just — let's just move on. She's nonresponsive."

"Maybe she's in shock?"

"No. I see — oh *shit*." A silence. "Hold on a second."

Another two shots crack the air.

Above you, two lights wink out, like stars.

"Alright. *Now* let's move on."

The truck rumbles forward. You follow them.

For the next hour the truck creeps along streets, killing your friends, and taking note of where survivors are. You take note of them too, and you communicate this to the collective.

Finally, the green truck arrives at what looks like a basecamp, and slows.

Turn to page 79.

You deke around the infected man. He makes a half-hearted attempt to cut you off but you are much faster. He turns, however, and follows you as you race to the tree.

The shadows of more figures appear. Where are they coming from? It's as if one of them sent out a signal.

Without stopping, you make the leap from lawn to bark. From experience, you know that the slightest hesitation in climbing a tree means a hasty, inelegant descent with sometimes torn claws and an even more brutal loss of dignity.

You climb up the tree and onto the branch where your girlfriend balances.

She looks down with widening eyes as more and more infected arrive. They paw at the tree uncoordinatedly, reaching up, trying to grab her tail, which she lifts high.

The choir of panting grows louder. All these open, slick mouths with rotted teeth, shining wetly underneath you. It's almost mesmerizing.

Your girlfriend meows at you, to catch your attention. You look over.

She wants you to follow her lead. Her claws extend and grip the branch firmly. She half turns, and her tensed, hind legs tremble. Is she going to jump? What is she thinking?

She leaps!

And lands on the head of one of the infected!

Without stopping, she immediately leaps to another head! Then a shoulder! Then a head again! In this way, like a skipping rock, she makes her way out through the herd of infected and away.

You are terrified. That was crazy.

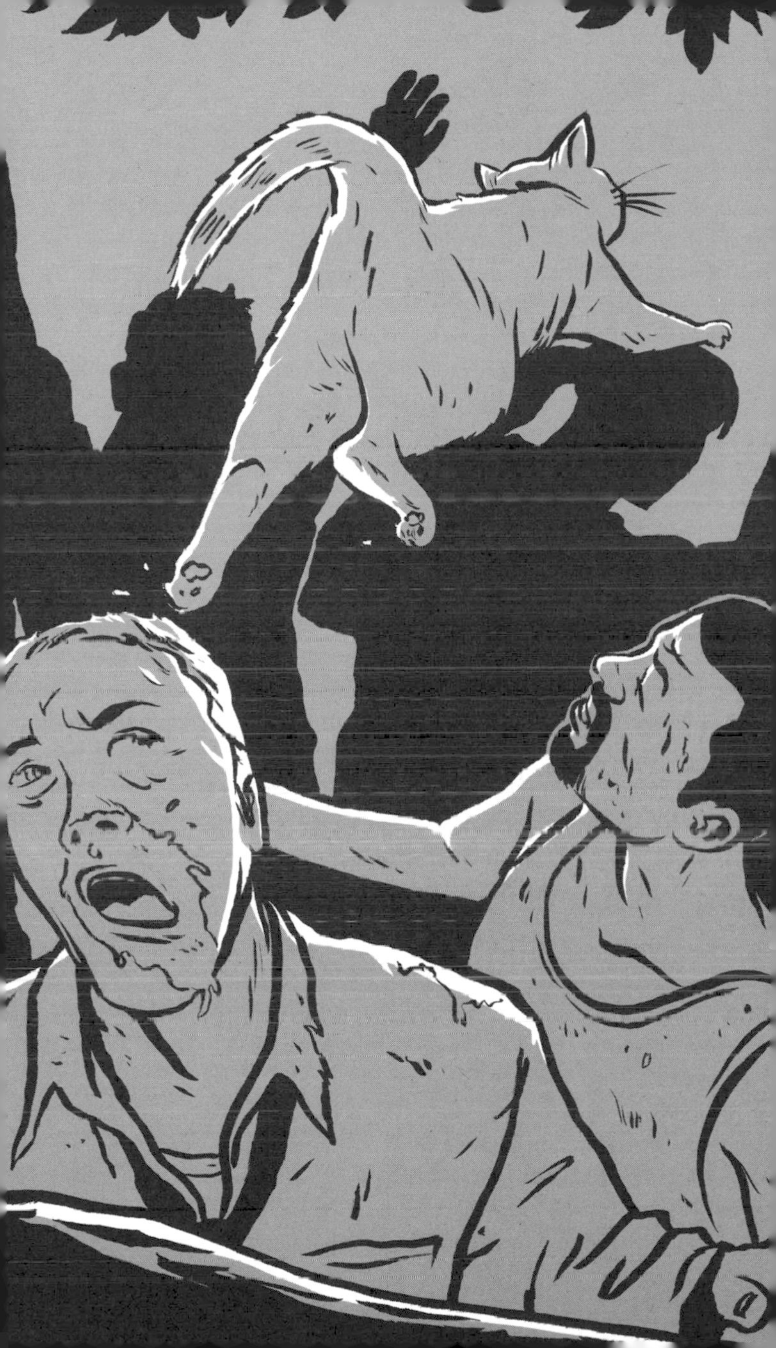

Some of the infected half turn, to see where she went. Others remain steadfastly focussed on you.

Okay. You have done this before. Made leaps you weren't sure you could land.

You go! Your paws land on the greasy hair of an infected, and you pivot off that to another head! Each head moves on its own, in its own direction, so this is a tricky thing, but you manage it, moving ever closer to the outside edge of the gathering.

It's all muscle memory. You just try to ride above the crest of your fear.

Finally you leap off a shoulder and onto the ground.

It feels so solid.

You scan the parking lot for a moment, looking for your girlfriend but she is hiding somewhere. By now, many of the infected have turned, and are coming after you.

You run away, out toward the street. They follow, the massive herd of them.

There are a few cars parked in the street. What you are looking for are options. The ability to move from one protected space to another. What you don't want is to get cornered.

As you duck under a car for temporary shelter, you hear something.

It is a low level hum which gets louder.

It's a truck, coming along the road.

You peer out. The infected, crossing the road to get to you have heard it too. They are stopping in the street as a large white light bathes them.

The truck stops.

"Holy shit!" you hear a man's voice. "We hit a pack of them! Permission to fire?"

"At will," another voice says.

Loud juddering booms accompany the sounds of infected humans being chopped apart. Heads fly off, chests burst with dark blood. Bodies crumple and collapse. Sparks glitter the dark pavement, and you don't move.

Finally, all's quiet and a blue smoke drifts across the road.

"Is that all of them?"

"Affirmative."

"Ready to move?"

"Let's go."

The truck begins to rev up again when a woman's voice pierces the air.

"Hey!" you see the woman behind the gate waving her arm.

"Sir — hold on!"

The truck quietens.

"Hey! We're over here!"

The large truck turns and rumbles into the parking lot. The man standing with a large mounted gun talks with the woman.

You venture out into the litter of infected body parts covering the road.

Nothing moves, and you move quickly through them.

Where is your girlfriend?

You scan the parking lot.

---

*If you want to check the tree again,
turn to page 145.*

*Or, if you think she might have headed back
towards the store, turn to page 214.*

The birds come flying in first.

They struggle, sluggishly to stay aloft, but they excel at pinwheeling down into tight, concentrated missles. Three of them hit the big bay window. Tiny suicidal bullets.

The girls inside jump, open-mouthed.

"What the fuck was that?"

The window, cracked, needs more pressure.

The bear clambers up and over the porch railing then dives headfirst into the glass. It comes down all around him, an ear-shattering waterfall of shards.

The girls are screaming.

Now the chipmunks, ferrets and the small quick animals, hop inside. And now you too. You struggle to get up and over the sill. Your body is all awkward angles.

Inside, the stranger is firing on the bear with her weapon, but the bear is unstoppable.

The girls retreat into the bedroom.

The bear presses its shoulder up against the bedroom door. It strains. The hinges creak. More pressure is needed.

You try to remember if there was a window in that room.

Could they escape?

You close your eyes and you see the cabin from the eyes of a fox on the other side. No window.

They're trapped.

The bear pulls back, then pushes again.

Everything is silent except for the low whine of strained metal.

Inside the room, you can hear the girls talking.

"Are you ready?"

"No. You?"

"No."

"Okay then. I'll do you first. And then me."

A pause.

"Okay."

"Awright."

"Wait! Wait!"

"What?"

"Kiss me."

A brief silence.

"Okay?"

"Okay."

There is a blast.

Then, a few moments later, another.

The big bear eases up its pressure.

You can sense the lives of the girls blinking out like two eyes closing.

Another vision — another cabin, not far. Your spies see three people inside. A man and a woman and a child.

Your night isn't over yet.

THE END

Even as infected humans stagger in your direction, you quickly run under a car and press up next to the comforting bulk of a wheel. You've never been overly fond of the smell of rubber, but over time, it's acquired a familiarity due to its association with particular cat-sized protected spaces. And it comforts you here now.

But not for long. Two of the infected drop to their knees and paw at you with blood-stained fingers.

Panicked, you move out of their reach, zipping underneath the other car. But before long, a third drops down. They're going to surround you. You can't keep this up forever.

Taking a chance, you dart out into the open, and look to see how your girlfriend is doing. Her momentum and claws have brought her up to the lowest branches, but it's not a very large tree, and the infected can probably reach her.

She knows it too, by the uneasy looks she's giving the few infected that have spotted her, and are closing in.

Behind you, the three infected that were pestering you have all realized you've left, and have turned their heads in unison, like a pack of dogs, toward you. They wrench themselves to their feet and reinitiate their stalk.

You look around.

Where can you go?

You see some bushes clumped between this parking lot and the one beside. You have managed to evade pursuing dogs in tight spaces before — maybe it'll work with these shambling idiots.

You hiss and howl at the infected to get their attention. Luckily, a couple of the figures near your girl-

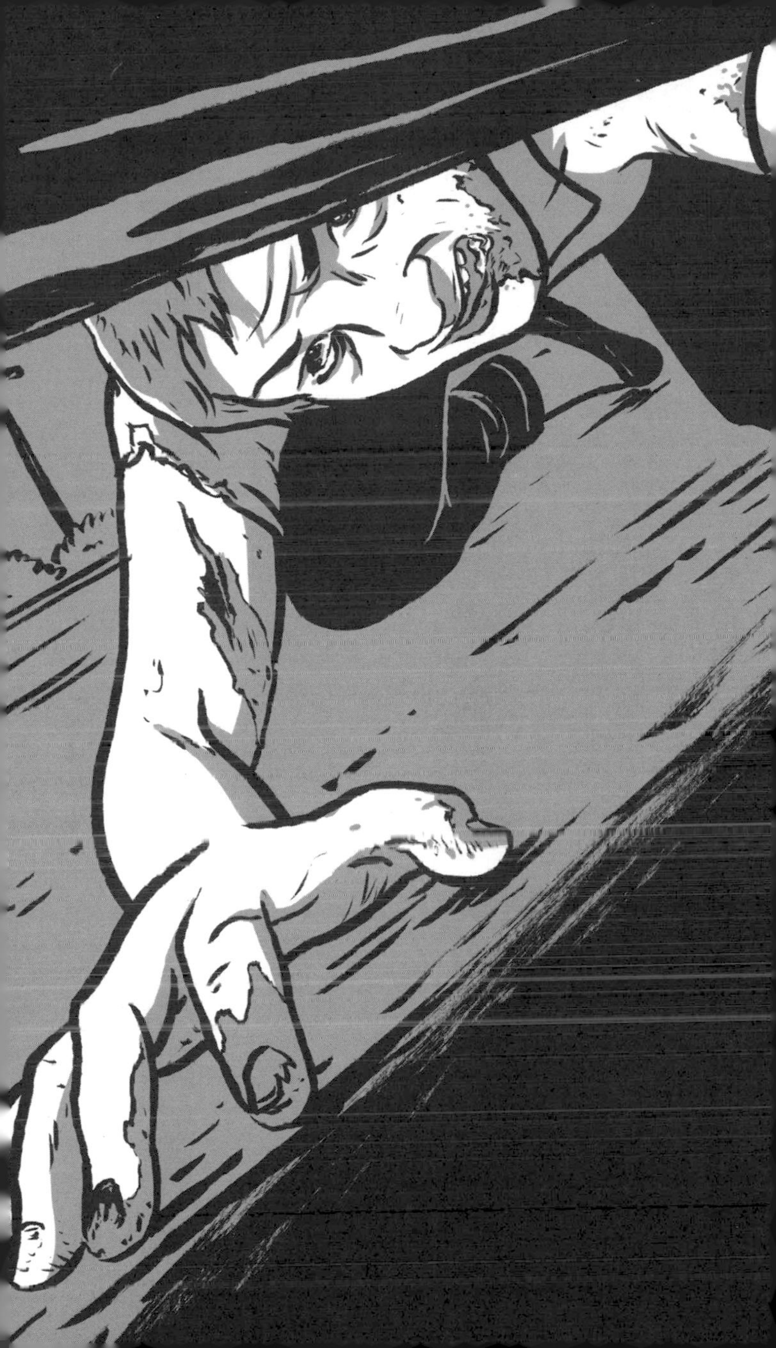

friend turn and refocus their attentions on you. The more you can get entangled in the bushes the better.

You move toward the line of dark green shrubbery, stopping once to make sure the infected are following.

When you're close enough, you squeeze between the tight branches of the bushes and out the other side.

But a movement catches your eye.

Something has followed you.

Something small, something fast.

Something that was in the bushes already when you arrived.

A squirrel grabs onto your tail and bites!

You try to shake it off but its grip is like the claws of kittens — needlelike and sharp. You turn and eventually manage to wrestle it off.

By now the infected have hit the bushes, falling into them, stampeding over one another to get to you.

Running away, you are terribly aware of the stinging pain in your tail, and a sudden wooziness. You might need to lie down for a bit.

If you decide — even in this nauseous state — to climb the tree to be with your girlfriend, turn to page 198.

If instead, you head back to the store and, behind the gate, take shelter near the door, turn to page 189.

You wait patiently at the door.

All the other animals, teeming from the forest, wait as well. A random wing flutters. A rabbit shifts. You gaze at the door and it's almost as if you can see through it. You see the girl, coming. Hear the radiating echo of her footsteps as she approaches. Feel the vibration under your feet.

"It's Holden!" the girl says, lilt of life in her voice.

"Don't!" the stranger, from behind her warns. "We don't know if it's him."

The door opens just a sliver.

The hundreds of others milling off the porch await your go-ahead.

"Holden?" the girl's eye appears in the crack.

You understand you must meow to get inside.

"Heh, hah," you manage to get out, flecking spittle.

"Oh shit," the girl says. "Oh no."

Digging your claws into the porch wood, you shoulder into the door, widening the opening. You manage to get your shoulders through before the girl realizes what's happening.

"Oh no!"

Go now, you say to the others.

The bear, spearhead of your herd, moves onto the porch and noses the big bay window.

For a few moments you see from his point of view. Lit cabin room. The girls, by the door, arms levered against it. Little orange cat halfway through the gap between doorframe and door.

"Fuck!" the stranger says. "He's getting in!" You hear her dully, through the window. You watch as the stranger backs up, then throws her entire body weight at the door.

You watch as the little orange cat is *cut in half*.

A wave of nausea.

You claw on the floor. You look up at the girls.

Screaming. One of the girls is screaming. The girl is screaming. They are backing up. Something is wrong with your body. You can only claw towards them, dragging yourself forward one arm at a time.

A crash of glass distracts them. The bear smashes through the window!

More screaming.

"What is that?! What is that?!!"

The stranger lifts her weapon, fires at the bear. He doesn't feel it. He takes her down. Climbs on top of her so she can't move. Begins gnawing on her shoulder.

In her panic, the girl has fallen. You manage to claw up to her face. You bite into her neck.

From the corner of your eye, you see the stranger. Her one unpinned arm raises the weapon. She aims it at you. You pause your munching and look at her.

But... she isn't looking at you. She is looking at the girl. And the girl is looking at her.

The girl nods. The weapon moves away from you, and lifts slightly, so now it's aimed at the girl's face.

There is a blast.

The bear looks over.

The girl is gone. The cat is also gone.

The one underneath will turn soon.

Love is spreading like a furious rainstorm, getting everyone wet!

THE END

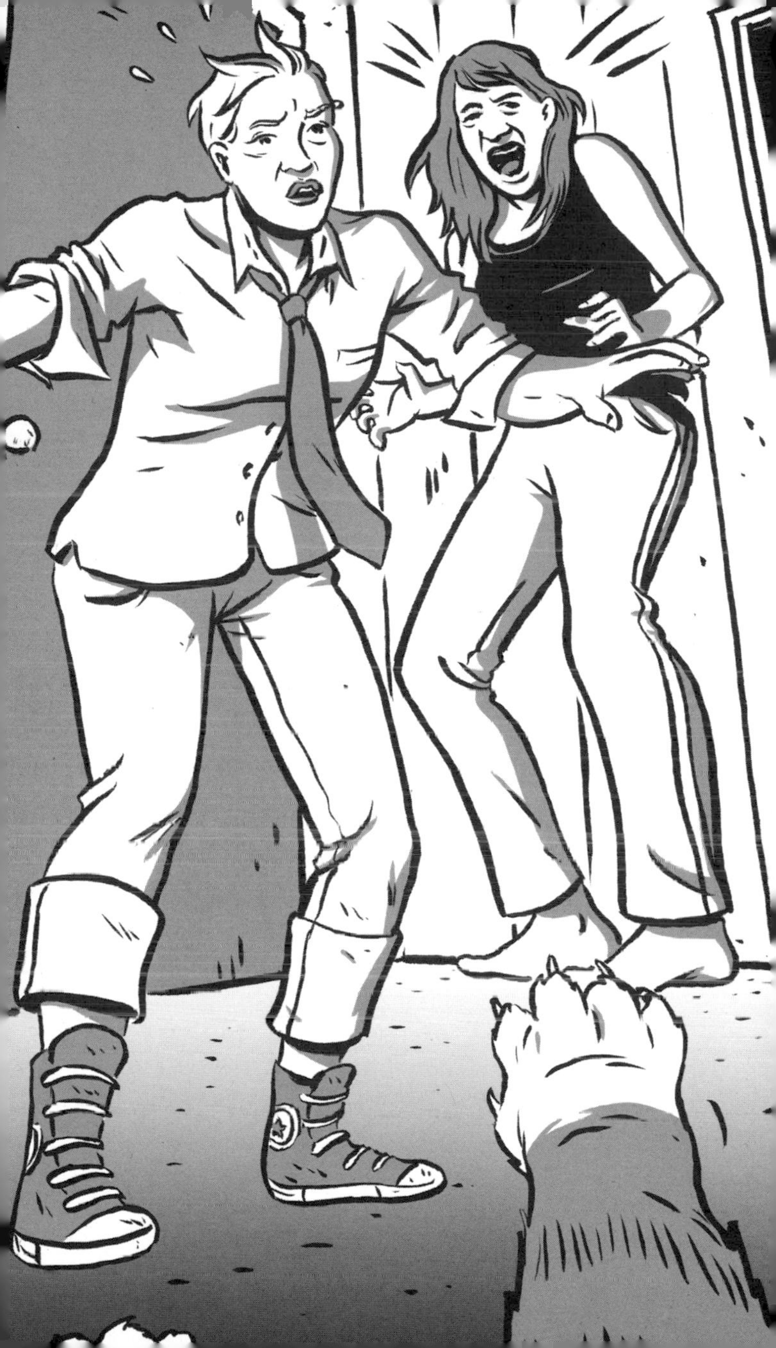

It begins as a hiss. This noise that seethes from you.

With a yowl, you leap on the man!

Who is he? To invade your house, your family, your territory?

You claw your way up his clothes to his face, swinging your claws, batting at his nose.

The man grabs you, tries to pull you off, but your claws are sunk deep into his jacket.

Behind you, footsteps. Then the stranger's voice.

"Move, kitten!"

"Don't shoot him!" the girl yells.

Finally, the man wrenches you off. Fabric rips underneath your claws.

As you fly through the air, you attempt to rotate, spin, to minimize your chances of injury when you land. You watch as the stranger raises her shotgun at the invading man.

A bright white flash and a deafening blast and the man is pushed back. He drops.

You hit the wall awkwardly, then fall with a thud.

"Ah, fuck!" the man whimpers. "Fuck!" He begins to cough.

It takes you a moment to find your feet again.

"Stay down!" the stranger warns. She reaches into her pocket and reloads the weapon.

Outside, the sound of the blast echoes through the woods.

"I'm not — " the man says, unable to breathe, clutching his chest, "I'm not going anywhere."

You hear the distinct sound of feet on the porch. Two shadows shuffle into view at the now open window.

"Hah, hah." The sound soughs out between the

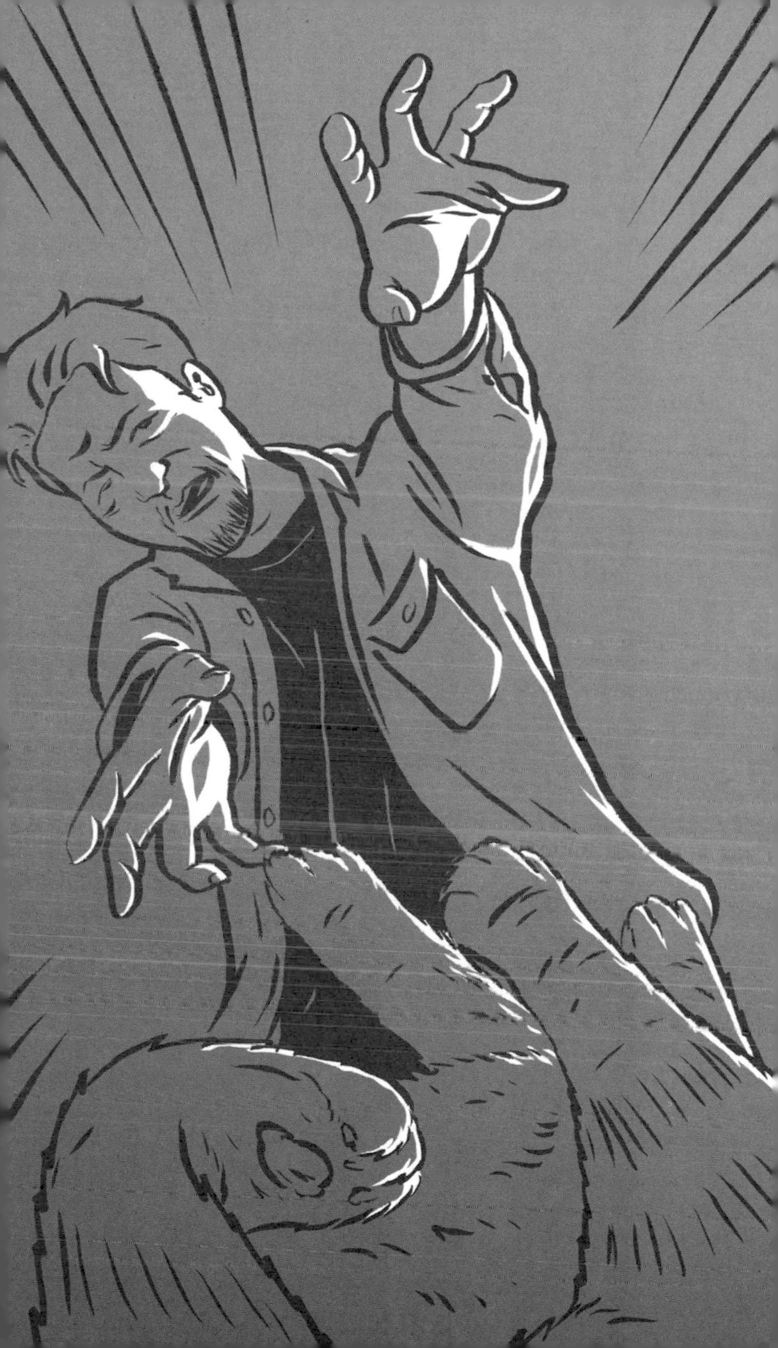

shadow's rotting teeth as it stumbles in over the windowsill.

"Julie," the stranger whispers. "Grab Holden. Now! We gotta go!"

The girl wraps her arms around you, gently but firmly, and lifts you into the air.

"Don't — " the man says, blood spittling from his lips, "Don't go. Don't leave me here."

The girls don't say anything as they open the cabin door and rush outside, leaving the man to his friends.

Turn to page 240.

Though the asphalt under your feet is spinning, you manage to make it back to the store. You squeeze in through the bars of the gate and curl up against the door. You peer in past the glass but don't see anyone who can let you in.

In the parking lot, infected have followed you and are pressed against the gate. Their collective pants unnerve you. They claw through the bars, but you are just inches out of reach.

You close your eyes for a moment. You are having difficulty staying conscious. Your head bumps against the door, and that knocks you back awake. But for that moment   you had the impression that you were not alone. That others walked with you, struggled with you. You had the faint grasp of an allegiance that was waiting for you.

Then, from inside the store — a movement. A pink blanket is flopped over and the younger girl sees you. She looks around, then gets up.

She pads over to you on socked feet. Looking around once more, she unlocks the door and pulls it open just wide enough for you to get in.

"Katie!" the mother's sharp voice calls from inside the store. "What are you doing?!"

"C'mon in kitty," the little girl says, as you crawl inside.

The woman comes running.

"I told you!" she's yelling. "What did I tell you?!"

"It's okay, Mom. It's the cat, from before. It's okay."

The woman grabs the little girl's arm and yanks her away.

"No. You don't *know* this cat. You don't know what he could have!"

The woman bends down and grabs you around the waist.

"No!" the little girl screams.

"He's gotta go out! He's gotta go!" The woman pushes open the front door, and, suddenly confronted by the flailing arms and panting mouths of the infected outside, stops in shock.

"Oh, god."

This is when you bite her in the forearm.

The woman screams and yanks you off, throwing you against the gate. Quickly, she shuts the door, and falls to the floor, clutching her arm.

The infected immediately paw at you, but after a moment they stop. They're no longer interested in you.

Woozy, you black out again. But this time, in your reverie, you can sense the infected behind you, and farther out too. You can see more out in the parking lot, the ones surrounding your girlfriend in her tree. You want your girlfriend to join you. So she can feel like this. A pleasurable sense of community courses through you. A feeling you haven't felt since being back in your house with the family, when they were all at home and together.

When you come to consciousness again, you see the woman edging herself outside. She levels her gaze at you.

"You going to hurt me?"

You merely stare.

"I didn't think so."

The woman turns around. The older girl is there on the other side of the door holding hands with the younger one.

"Lock it behind me!" the woman says.

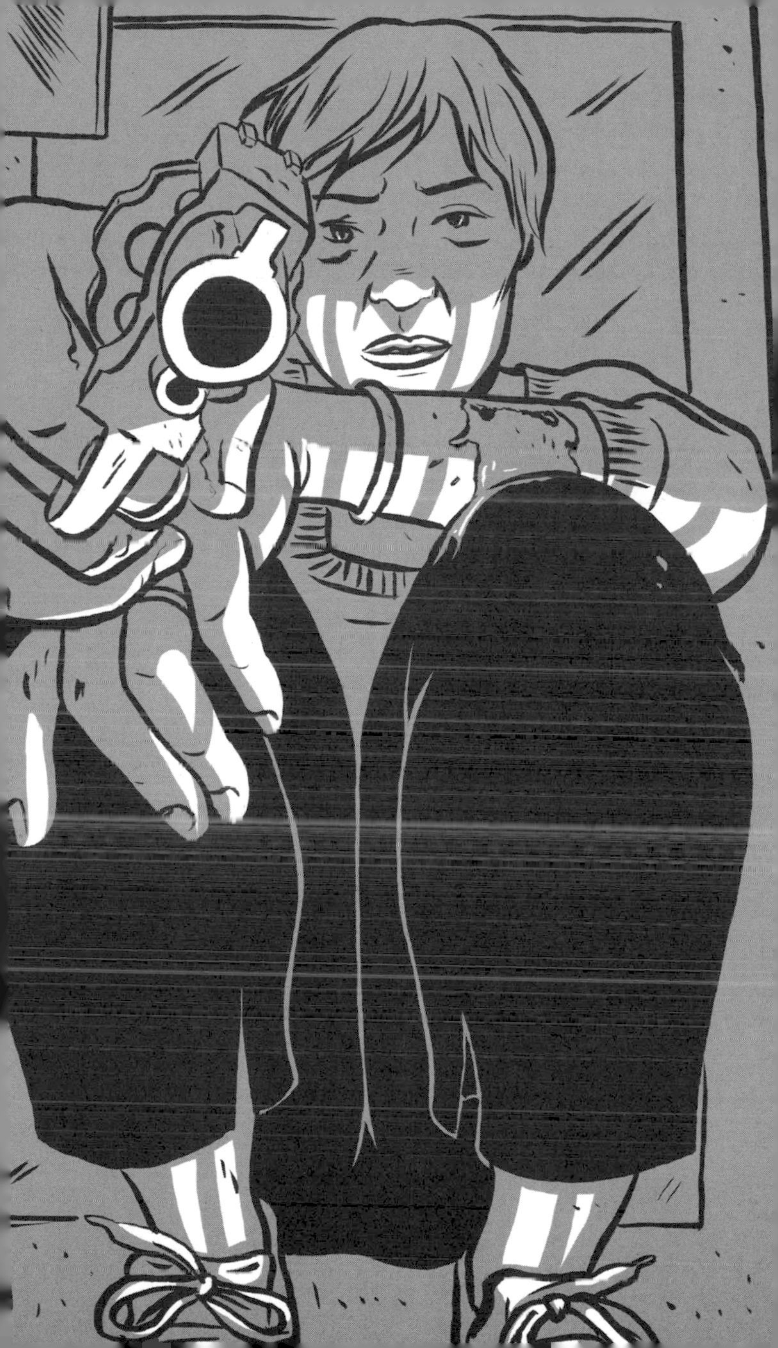

"Mommy!" both girls are crying, but do as she says.

"Stay here until help comes!"

"Mom, when's Dad getting here?" the older girl asks.

"Your father's — your father's not here," the woman says. She starts crying too. "I don't know where he is. He might not get here."

Now the woman turns back around to face you. She leans back against the glass door and slides down into a squat. She has something in her hands. It's the gun. She points it at you.

"I should kill you," she says. "Blow you away. For what you did."

"Mommy!" the girls are screaming at her, muffled behind the glass.

"Don't open the door to anyone!" the woman yells over her shoulder. Then, "Girls, look away! Cover your eyes!"

The woman glances over her shoulder to emphasize her point.

"Cover them!"

Behind her, the girls reluctantly cover their eyes with their hands. You see the older girl peek.

"I love you!" the woman says.

Then, she takes the gun and tucks it underneath her chin the way a bird will tuck its head under its wing. She is out of breath from all the yelling.

"Heh, hah," she pants. Then her head explodes.

The noise is very muted, somehow. Your ears twitch, and you see everything through a kind of haze. The woman falls to the ground and sprawls out before you. The gun clatters to her side as her arm falls.

The panting of the infected behind you mixes

with the sobbing of the girls inside.

A moment later, the older girl carefully unlocks the door and opens it just an inch. She glares at you.

You are going to bite her *too*.

But she's too fast. In a moment her thin arm darts out and retrieves the gun the woman was holding. The door closes again. For a second you consider charging the glass, breaking through to her, but you understand that in this form, you won't be able to penetrate it.

Outside, at the tree, you can feel your girlfriend fall to the ground and join the community.

The door opens again, just a little, just enough for the gun barrel to emerge. The girl sights down along the gun and her eyeball impales you with its gaze.

"Fuck you cat," the girl says.

Then a bullet impales your brain.

THE END

You leave the girls to their concerns and jump down from the counter.

The first room off the main one is markedly colder. Pallid light streams in from a tiny window. You venture onto the smooth tiles of the shower. A thin layer of dust covers everything and you leave the faintest of paw prints as you walk around.

Then you see it.

Yes.

The toilet.

And the cover is up.

Delicately, you jump up onto its smooth rim. Steadying yourself, you lean in and drink from the small pool of water. The water from a toilet is always more interesting. More flavourful.

You know that your family doesn't approve. This isn't something that you're supposed to do.

Everyone chides you if they catch you doing this. Except for the man.

One time he caught you in the home toilet and you winced, like he was going to yell, "No, Holden!"

But he didn't. He just laughed. He just backed off and said, "Don't worry, kid. I'm glad to know I'm not the only one with a drinking problem."

You think about the man. Big, bearded, comforting rumble of a voice. And what he became. Something else. Something you didn't recognize.

That was the moment everything changed.

When you've had your fill of water, you jump back down and return to the main room.

The stranger is still trying her phone.

Finally, she says, "Shit! This is ridiculous." Then she gets up and heads to the door.

"Where are you going?" the girl asks.

"I'm going to try the radio in the car for a bit. See if I can get more info about what's going on. Also, there's a shed I should look through. Sometimes my mom leaves some things out there. I might find something."

"Should you go by yourself?"

The stranger laughs.

"I'll be okay. No one knows we're out here. And I'll take the gun."

"Well. Okay. Be safe."

After the girls kiss goodbye, the stranger leaves and the girl stretches out on the couch. She begins to play a game on her phone, little bright flashing gems sparkling and cracking, but then shuts it off.

"God, I wish I had a book!" she says.

Always charmed by the prospect of an open lap and a possible nap, you jump up onto the couch.

"Then I wouldn't feel so guilty about having my phone on. Using up all the power. And I left my fucking charger back home in my bag."

You walk onto the girl's thighs, then over to her belly.

You look at her. She looks at you.

You can see the exhaustion sitting on her shoulders.

You've only ever seen her this tired a few times in her life. You are sad to see it again. You crawl over her breasts to her face and smell her lips.

The girl laughs. She gives you a kiss on the nose and runs her fingers along the edges of your ears.

You smell her mouth again. She hasn't had any food recently either.

That doesn't bode well if the girl isn't eating anything.

196

The girl loves to eat.

You place your paws on her chest and start to knead her shirt.

The girl giggles.

"Holden! I'm ticklish!"

You continue to knead. The movement is familiar. The girl closes her eyes and smiles.

Her stress dissipates like a morning fog in the sun.

Finally you put your head down. The girl is beginning to relax. She's going to sleep. She needs to. You decide to sleep as well.

Fall asleep over to page 165.

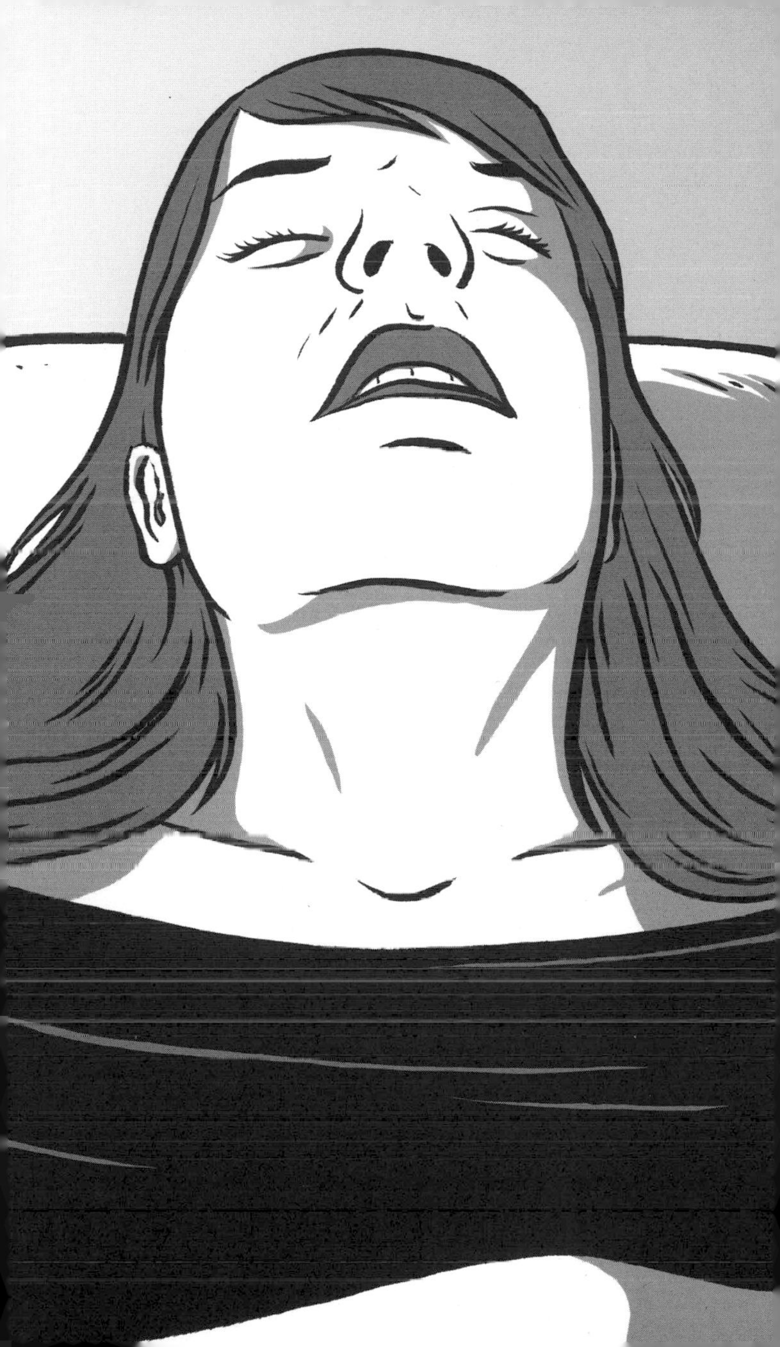

You run back to the tree. By now, more infected have gathered, but you gallop between their lumbering legs and scramble up. You see the branch your girlfriend is on and make your way there.

In your life, getting up a tree has always been easy. Getting down is a lot harder. But you don't think about that now as you venture out onto the branch.

Your girlfriend stands balanced on it, staring down at the slavering mass below. They reach up and try to grab her. Smartly, she keeps her tail high in the air.

She meows a greeting at you, and comes toward you, but suddenly one hind leg slips! She works to regain her balance, but she's slipping off one side! You run over, practically slipping off yourself, and you reach out! She's falling, but manages to sink her claws into your arm in desperation.

Amazingly, it doesn't hurt.

Why doesn't it hurt?

You drop your own body down the other side, as a counterweight, and as you descend, your girlfriend is lifted back up onto the branch. But as she finds her footing and retracts her claws, you suddenly no longer have the strength to pull your*self* up. Maybe you never had it.

You drop down to the grass.

The infected come at you.

You meow at them, managing to capture their attention. As you lead them away, toward the parked cars, you see your girlfriend jump down from the tree and run back to the store.

Then you are suddenly clobbered by vertigo.

You drop down onto your face. Dumbly, you try to make it to your feet, but you black out for a mo-

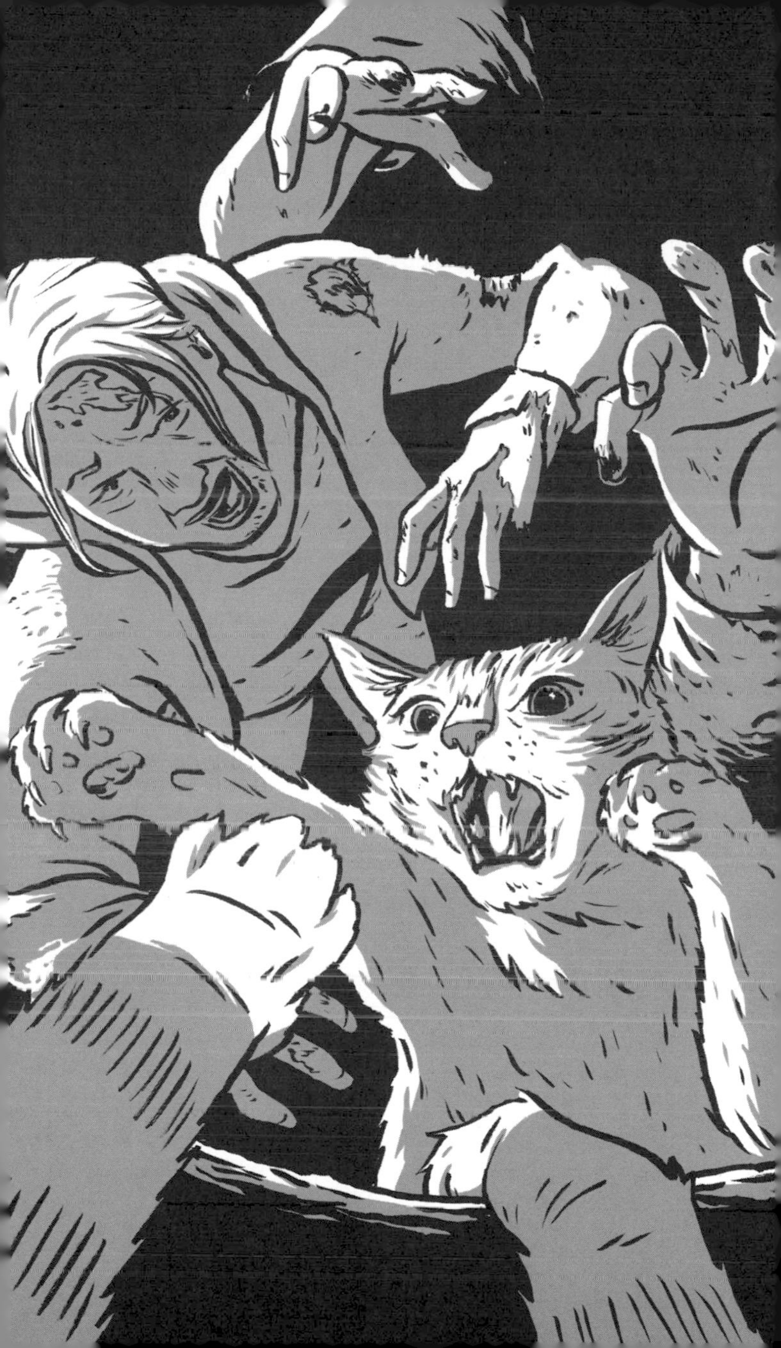

ment.

Or it might have been more than a moment. You're not sure.

But when you come to, you have a marvellous feeling in your heart.

You reach out with your senses and the way you could almost see smells in the past is now how you can see your fellow brethren, standing around the parking lot, their chorus of panting like comforting sighs.

They all know, as you do, that there is food, expansion, love, inside the store.

You want to lead them to it.

You stagger over to the storefront, slip in through the gate and press your head against the glass door.

The infected follow you, though their human bodies are too big to get through.

"Oh god, mommy!" one of the girls sees you.

The other girl is stroking an off-white cat.

That cat.

She looks familiar.

Your mind claws for the memory of the relationship.

In a moment, your dazed mind remembers.

She's your girlfriend.

When you get inside, you're going to eat her first.

THE END

You run back into the bedroom and hide under the bed. All this is terrifying. The man, the sound of the window breaking. Everything you know has been turned upside-down in the last couple of days and you are ready to break down, ready to spend the rest of your life underneath this bed. You close your eyes.

"Get out! Get out!" the stranger yells from the front room. "I'll shoot!"

"Don't shoot!" the man pleads. "The sound will bring them!"

"What were you thinking!?" the girl screams. "Crashing our window? What the fuck?"

When you hear the girl's voice, you open your eyes. Is she okay? She is the last thread of normalcy in your life. Slowly, you move over to the bedroom doorway.

The man stands, arms up. The stranger has the shotgun aimed at him. The girl is against the wall, close to you.

At the window, two figures come into view. You hear them before you see them — the awkward foot-steps on the porch, the laboured breathing.

"Hah, hah," the figures sigh.

The man turns his head to see, then, grabs at the stranger's weapon.

"Hey!" she yells. "Don't!"

A fiery blast over his shoulder as they struggle for it!

More loud noise! Your eyes clamp shut.

"Oof!"

Your eyes pop open. The man kicks the stranger in the stomach, then turns the shotgun on her!

"Back!" Get back!"

The stranger retreats, flattening herself against

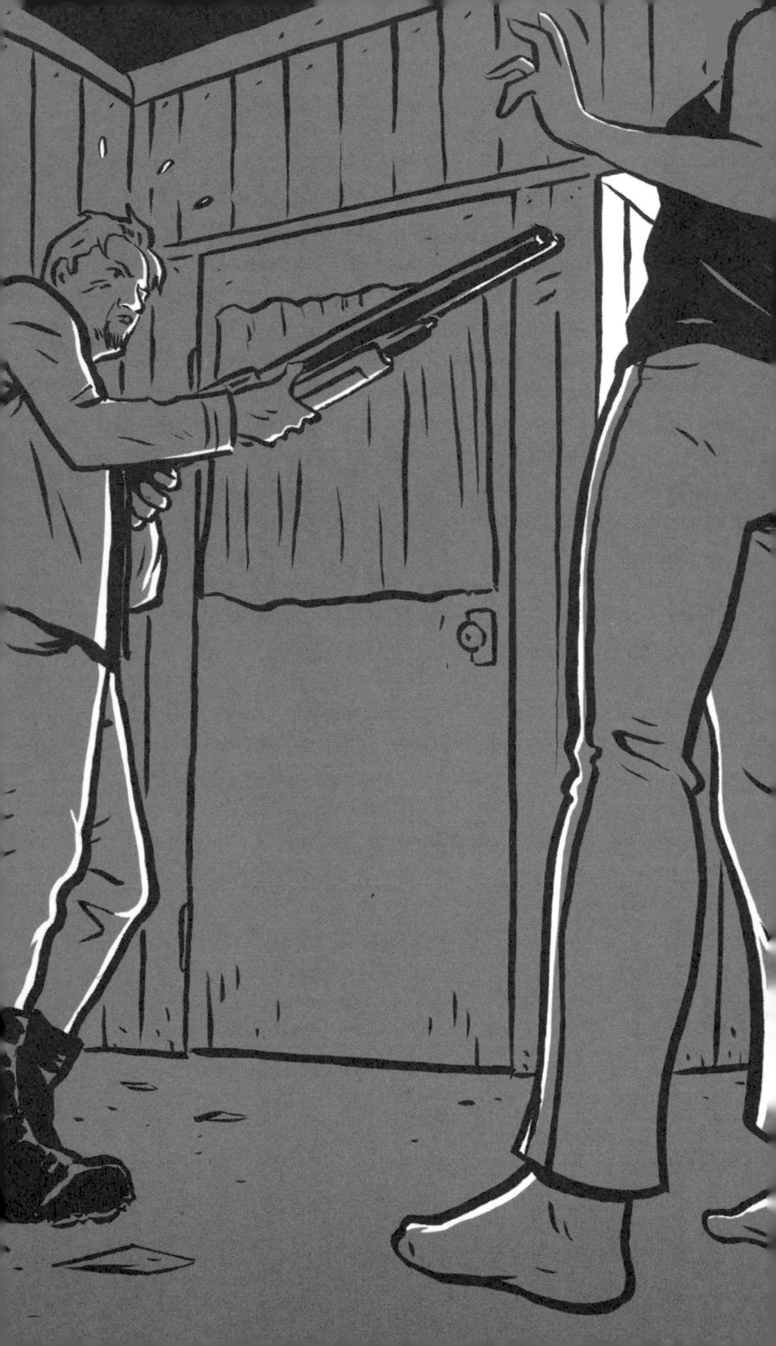

the wall beside the girl. Both raise their arms.

"Hah," one of the figures at the window begins coming over the sill. The remaining glass sticks out like jagged teeth. He stabs himself on them, small shards cracking and falling, but pays it no mind.

The man spins, aims at the shadowy figure.

"Shoot!" the stranger whispers.

The man is frozen.

"Shoot him!"

The figure is inside. His strange smell drifts over to you. Your nose twitches. He smells like the man, back in the house, where this all started.

"Kevin, stay back!" the man says.

The stranger taps the girl on the shoulder and points to you.

The girl nods and picks you up.

As the man is transfixed on the shambling intruder, you and the girls move slowly to the cabin door.

"Kev, don't! Please! Don't make me shoot you!"

Outside, the girls run to the car.

Turn to page 240.

"Well," the girl says, "at least we know he's still alive."

The stranger flops onto the couch, still pushing buttons. "Or," she says, "that was like, his dying call. Calling to tell me he loves me."

"Oh god!" the girl says. She sits down beside the stranger. "Really?! Is that how it sounded? That he was dying?"

"I'm kidding," the stranger says, "Don't freak out."

"You're kidding?"

"Kinda."

The girls sit in silence for a moment, lost in their thoughts. The stranger finally sets her phone down, shaking her head. You decide to join them on the couch and you drop down off the counter, and walk over. One of your favourite things is to wedge yourself between two people. The energy that passes between them is wonderful and it warms you up. Like the sun warms a black driveway on a summer day, so it stays warm even into the cool of the night.

"Amanda?" the girl says.

"Yah."

"Are you afraid to die?"

"Me? I don't know. Maybe. You?"

"Not so much for myself. You know I told you — well, a few years back I had like, a suicide attempt, right?"

"Yah, you told me."

"So like, I'm not afraid to die," the girl says. "But I'm afraid for my family. I don't want them to die painfully. I don't want my dad to like — be alone. In the house like that."

You snuggle into the space between the girls'

thighs and close your eyes. The girl laughs.

"Good old Holden," she says. She looks at the stranger. "Priorities, right? Not a worry in the world."

The stranger stands up. You look up at her. Is everything okay? Why did she have to go and disturb the beautifully delicate equilibrium everyone had established on the couch?

"What is it?" the girl asks.

"I gotta do something."

"What?"

"*Anything.* I just gotta — get up, do *something.* There's like, a shed, back down the drive a little bit. Sometimes we store stuff in there. I want to see if there's anything we can use."

"Well, I'll come with you."

"No, it's okay. Stay here with Holden. I'll be back soon. I just need to stretch my legs. I'm getting cabin fever."

"After one day?"

"No, it's — I'm sorry. I'm just restless and stressed out. I gotta feel like I'm doing something."

"All right. Well, take the gun."

The stranger nods and picks up the shotgun from the countertop.

"Don't go too long," the girl says.

"I won't," the stranger says. She goes over and gives the girl a hug and kiss. "See you soon."

The girl sits in silence on the couch for a bit and then checks her phone.

"I can't believe how late it's gotten," she says to you. "We didn't even *do* anything."

You and the girl gaze out the big bay window. Fleecy clouds litter the deep blue sky. The day has passed into mid-afternoon very quickly.

You crawl into the girl's lap and stretch out. She looks down at you and smiles.

"Haha, oh Holdy." She takes her hand and rubs it up and down your chest, feeling your rib cage and the extra soft white fur that overlays it. Then she lets her hand rest there for a moment.

"Let me see if I can feel your heart."

You look at the girl. She has her eyes closed. She is concentrating intently. Finally she opens her eyes and smiles at you again.

"You've got a great heart, Holden."

Then she takes a deep breath and lets out a long sigh.

"I should probably — "

The girl looks up at the window and you see her eyes are now brimming with water. She takes her phone and turns it on. She presses a few things and then says, "Hi Mom. Hi Dad. Hey Jason. It's me."

The girl blinks and the water in her eyes spill like raindrops down her cheek.

"I'm here with Holden. Holden's with me," the girl turns the phone to you. You see a picture of a cat in the phone! "Say hi, Holden."

Who is the cat?

The girl turns the phone back to herself. By now the girl's tears are falling on you. You move to a dryer spot.

"So I'm hoping you'll get this. Through some like, miracle, you'll get this recording. I just want to tell you all that I love you. That's all."

"Thank you being the best kind of family. I was having a really hard time a few years ago, and you walked with me through it. You stuck it out with me and I really — "

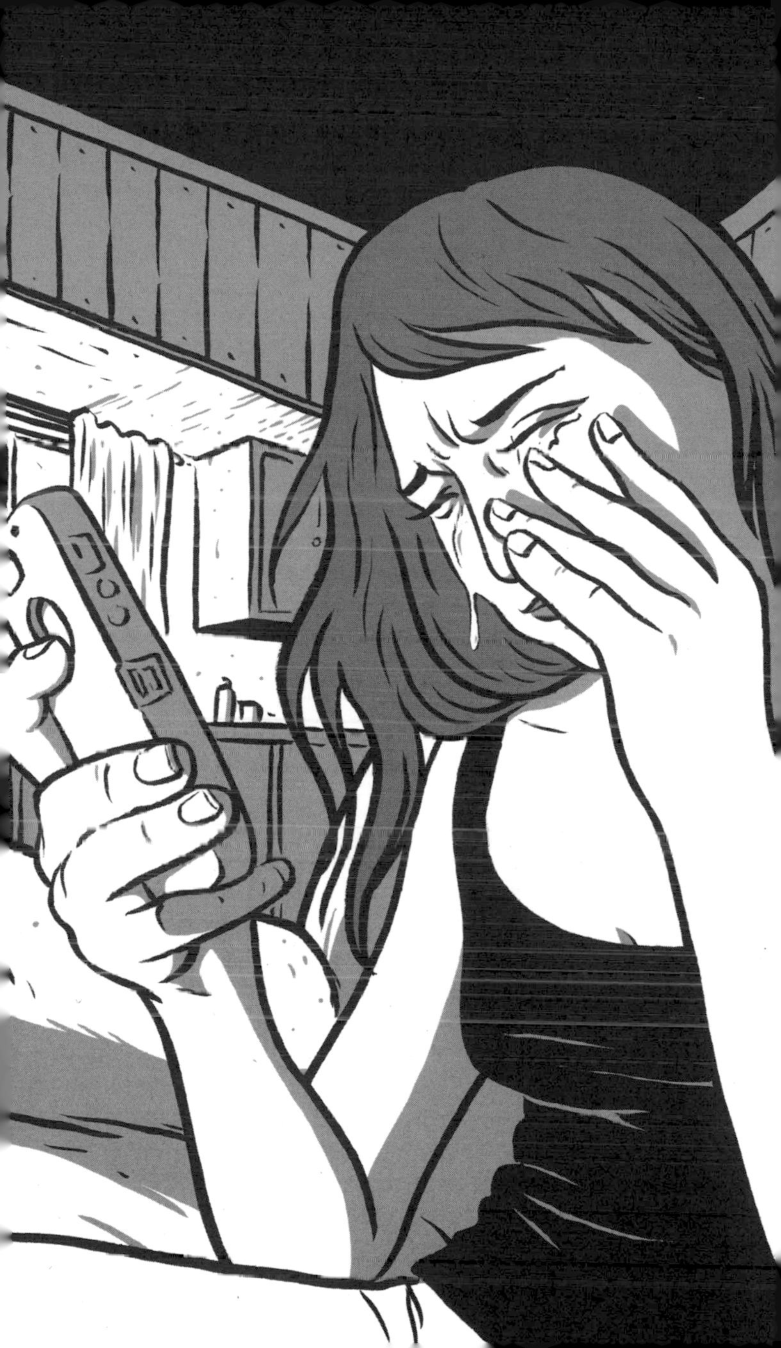

208

The girl sobs here. She clutches you and puts the phone down for a second. What's going on? Why is she so upset? You hate it when she's this upset.

"I really appreciate it," the girl continues, biting back a sob. "That's all. I don't know what's going to happen. It seems like the end of everything."

The girl takes a few deep breaths and wipes her eyes with her knuckles.

"What else? I was going to tell you classes are going okay. I have one — abnormal psych, that's fascinating. I've met a few people that I really like. And ah — " The girl blushes. "I've got like, this girlfriend now. Well, I don't know if she — " The girl halts. "I was hoping you all would meet her. I really like her! We're like, new."

Outside, the sky is getting almost imperceptibly darker.

"Anyway, that's all. That's all I really wanted to say. That I love you all. That I want you to know that. That I hope to see you all again sometime. Maybe in another time. Another place."

More tears.

"I think I gotta go. My battery's dying. And I don't have my charger with me. Say bye Holden." The girl turns the phone to you. There's that cat again!

"I love you! Bye!"

The girl shuts off the phone and then sobs.

She cries for a good long while and then lies back on the couch.

The room gets darker and darker.

In a while, the girl gives off little snores. And soon you do too.

Turn to page 165.

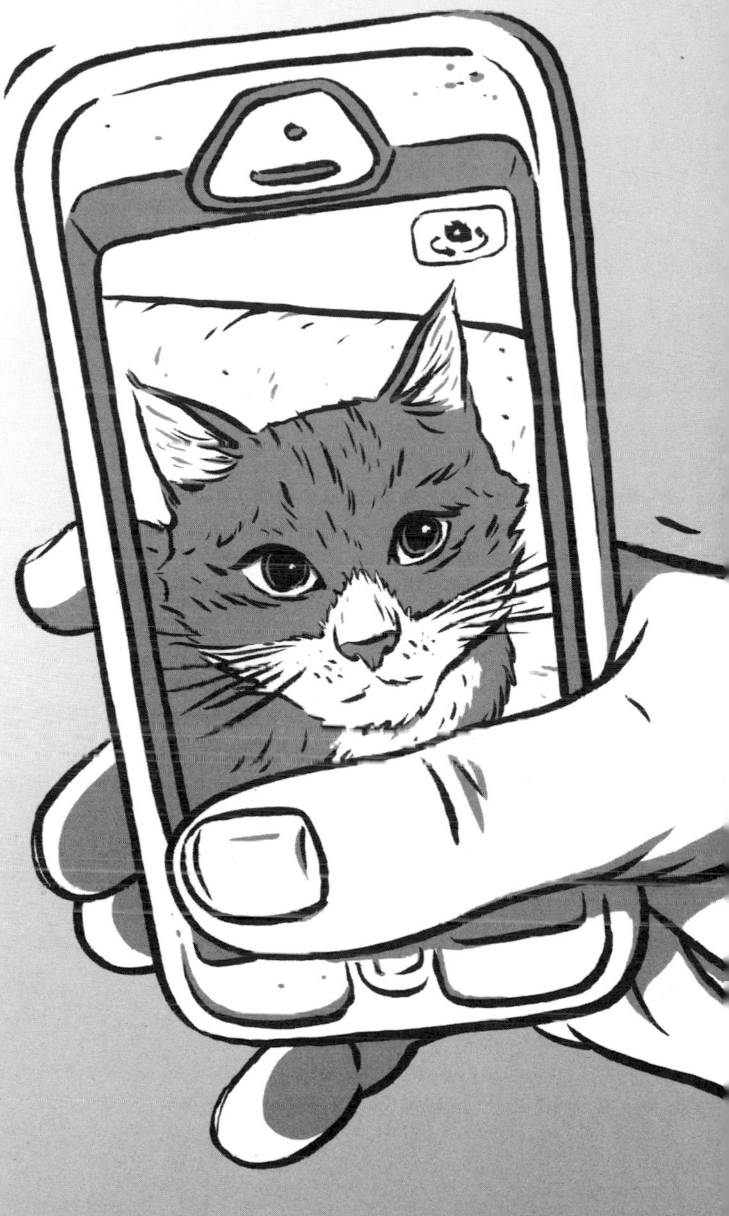

You move toward the mouse. It starts to shit itself, rears up on its hind legs and puts its puny arms out in front of it. You bite down on the whole of it, take it into your mouth. It struggles inside your mouth. Your rough tongue keeps it in place as your teeth sink into it. Its blood mingles with your saliva. Then you drop it.

The mouse falls, stunned.

It shudders a little, then is still.

"Is it dead?" the man asks. He steps out from behind the camera.

The woman looks closely.

"I don't think so. I think this is the infection. We have to wait for it to take hold."

The woman slides the cover of your cage open a little and drops another mouse in with you!

By this time the first mouse you bit is coming around. You are starting to sense it. You decide to leave the second mouse for the first one to love.

Seeing you, the second mouse tries to hide behind the first one. Then, suddenly, the mouse you turned leaps on the second one!

"This is so creepy," the man says.

"We've got our own private little zombie apocalypse happening here. Right before our eyes."

"At least we won't run out of test subjects. We can always make *more*."

The woman licks her lips.

"Let's try him with something bigger."

The woman leaves the room for a few moments, coming back with two large men in black T-shirts. Between them, they have hold of a slow, smiley man in a grey shirt and pants. They escort him into another cell and sit him down on a chair. Then the black T-

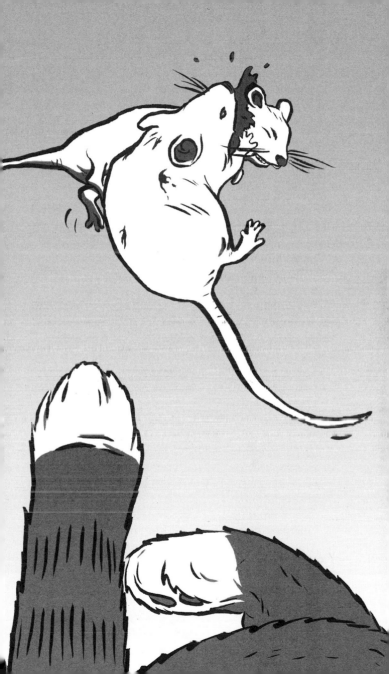

shirts leave.

"Hi Randall," the woman says sweetly.

"Hi Miss," Randall smiles at her.

"No Hi for me Randall?" the man asks.

Randall looks away.

"Well fuck you too, Randall," the man says. The woman laughs.

Randall frowns, then he sees you.

"Kitty!" Randall says, delightedly.

"Would you like to play with the kitty, Randall?" the woman asks.

"Oh yah!"

The woman comes over to you and lifts your cage up, bringing you over to Randall's cell. Opening his door, she leaves your cage on the floor. She closes Randall's cell door and pushes a button. A little green light on the handle blinks on.

Randall comes over and lifts the cover off your cage.

"Oh, miceys too!"

He reaches in and starts stroking you excitely.

If you decide to bring love to Randall, turn to page 218.

If instead you decide not to infect him at this time turn to page 135.

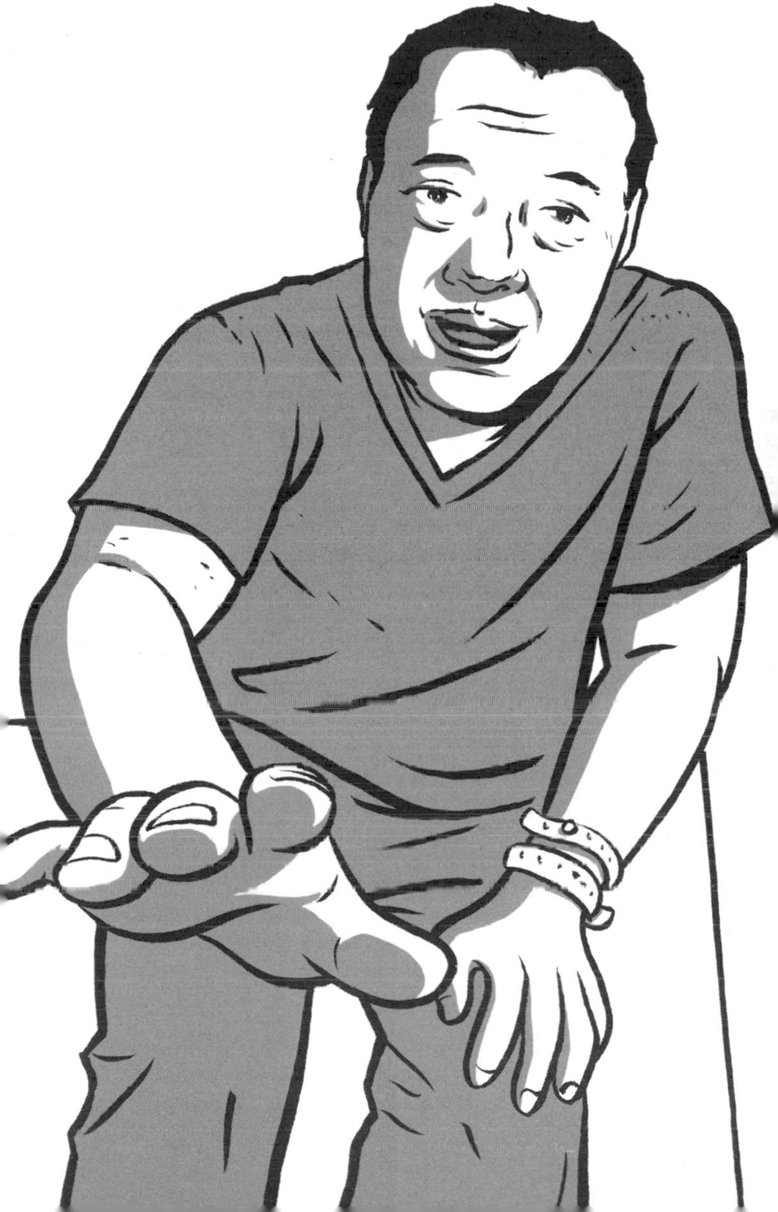

You make your way back to the store and hide underneath one of the parked cars. The woman leans against the bars of the gate and talks to the man on the truck.

"Ma'am, how are you doing?" he asks her.

"We need help. What's going on?"

"Ma'am, we aren't sure. As far as we know there's some kind of viral outbreak —"

"Are they zombies?" the woman interrupts.

"Now," the man hesitates. "We're not calling them zombies."

"They *look* like zombies."

"At this point we don't know."

"I saw you shoot them," the woman points at the bodies covering the road. "You shot them like zombies."

The man falters.

"Whatever's making these people sick is also causing them to attack others. We have a duty to prevent further attacks."

You move from underneath the car to underneath the green truck. It idles at a low throb. Normally you are terribly uncomfortable going underneath vehicles that are making any sounds. It usually means that they're moving, have moved very recently, or are about to move, and that makes them very dangerous. But you really want to find your girlfriend, and you haven't found her anywhere.

"You said they're sick. So is there a cure?"

The man shakes his head. "We don't know. It's too soon. Right now we're just gathering folks who aren't sick."

"So we can come with you?"

The man shakes his head again.

"No, not with us. Not right now. We're just here to remove threats, but we can send a personnel vehicle to pick you up at dawn. Can you be prepared to go then? How many of you — "

You see your opportunity. You run from the green truck toward the gate.

"Whoa! Ma'am, get back!"

The woman jumps as you dart between her legs into the store.

"Ahh! Don't shoot! Don't shoot!" the woman screams at the man, throwing her arms out.

You run into the store and look around, desperate. You were hoping you wouldn't be noticed. Suddenly, a small pair of arms wraps themselves around you. The little girl envelops you.

"Ma'am — find that cat! Might be infected!"

The woman runs into the store and spots you.

"Katie! Drop that now!"

"No! He's mine!"

"Drop him!"

"No!" The little girl is screaming in your ear. You wince, and fold your ears down protectively. You wish she would shut up.

"Daddy would never let *anyone* hurt him. Where's daddy?"

The woman stops, closes her eyes.

"Ma'am!" the man calls from outside. "Did you find him? If you get infected, we won't pick you up! Don't get bit! That's how it spreads."

The woman looks at you. "Let me see him," she says.

"No," the little girl is adamant. She squeezes you uncomfortably.

"I'm not going to hurt him — I just want to check

him for bites or scratches."

Reluctantly, the girl drops you. The woman approaches. You tense up. Should you run back out the front door? Your girlfriend doesn't appear to be in the store.

The woman squats and makes chucking noises with her tongue.

You wonder if she has food for you. You are so hungry and so thirsty.

You're tense, but you let the woman look you over, run her hands across your back.

"Katie," the woman says, "C'mere and shine your flashlight over him."

You don't like the bright light. You don't like being examined.

"Ma'am," the man calls from the front. "I need to get going. Are you okay?"

The woman finishes her examination and then goes out front.

"We're good. The cat is clean!"

"You won't be able to bring the cat along with you when we come to pick you up. Humans *only*."

The woman nods.

"There's three of us. Myself and my two daughters."

"Be ready at sunrise. We're going to send a bus."

The woman nods.

"Good luck," the man says. The green truck roars into movement and exits the parking lot, trundling down the road.

The woman closes the door and leans back against it.

"Maybe he's a sign," she says, pointing at you. "He's a messenger. We might just be fine. We might just get out of here."

"Mom, where's Dad?" the older girl asks her.

The woman sighs and slides down to the ground.

"Is he dead?" the older girl persists.

The woman is silent for a second, then says, "I don't know. We were texting yesterday. Then the texts just stopped coming. He was — " The woman catches herself, then relaxes. "Well I suppose he wouldn't mind if I told you now. He was at the toy store, picking up your birthday present. He texted me to make sure that he was getting what you wanted. But then the texts stopped. I don't know why. And then the news. And things going crazy. And that part of town was particularly crazy. I just — well, I had to protect you girls!" Tears spring from the woman's eyes. "I don't know where he is."

The little girl strokes you, hugs you.

"Mom, how long till dawn?"

The woman looks at her wrist.

"We have about three hours. You girls should go back to bed."

You squirm free of the girl. That was nice, but you want to find your girlfriend. As the woman and her daughters lie down, you search the store but there is no sign of her.

Suddenly you are filled with despair. Is she dead? Is she one of them?

You jump up onto the front window display and look outside.

Fatigued, you fall asleep, despite yourself.

___

Turn to page 224.

Arching your neck, you bite into Randall's arm!

"Argh!" he screams and backs away. "Bad! Bad kitty!"

He turns to the woman and man.

"Kitty bit me!"

"Poor Randall," the woman says soothingly. "Poor Randall."

Randall sits down on the chair and holds his arm. Blood drips on the pure white floor of the cell. Randall makes little whiny noises.

At your feet, both mice have now turned.

You jump out of the cage, and look at Randall. He squeals and gets up, goes to the cell door. He pushes against it.

"Lemme out! Lemme out miss!"

The woman shakes her head.

"Poor Randall," she coos. "Sit down Randall. Sit down."

He pounds on the plexiglass. Starts screaming. You wander over to the other side of the cell and settle on the floor, watching him.

"Lemme out!" he keeps pounding against the door, but then falters. He seems to be out of breath.

Then he slides down to the floor and sits, panting hard.

"Randall?" the woman calls to him. "How are you feeling?"

He looks at the woman, bleary-eyed.

"Not so good miss. I'm kinda feeling bad."

"How bad? Do you feel like throwing up? Are you going to be sick?"

"No," he mutters, shaking his head. "Just bad."

Randall closes his eyes and leans back against the plexiglass.

The woman walks toward the cell.

"This seems to happen every time. Newly infecteds go catatonic for a short duration. We saw it with the mice."

When Randall comes to, he isn't much for talking. You sense him fully now. Somehow, you feel closer to him. Maybe it's because you were the one who turned him, who taught him love.

Randall pants at the woman and man.

"Randall?" the woman calls to him. She knocks on the plexiglass. "You there?"

Randall walks toward her, stopped by the glass.

"All right," the woman says to the man. "Let's make more. Let's measure them, before and after. Let's test pain tolerances, weight, stamina, everything. The whole shebang."

Over the next few hours, they bring more humans in and infect them in the other cells. Using the mice you turned, they infect even more creatures. Dogs, humans, fish. You sense them all. Through their eyes you even get a better sense of the layout of the building.

And then — a sudden realization.

There are a *lot* of you.

There are several guards, sure, and more outside the facility, but it's like a zoo. They rely so much on the cages. But cages aren't forever. Not the way love is.

Through your brethren, you know that a lot of the humans have gone to sleep. There are barracks at the facility, and many of them are in their own cages.

Now is the time.

The collective doesn't like this place. Like a cat hates a room it can't get into, the collective is deeply suspicious of this inaccessible facility. But now they are sending others to help you. They are coming.

You are unable to penetrate the plexiglass, but Randall has a chance.

Randall knows what he has to do. He starts throwing his body against the walls!

His body is breaking. His shoulder cracks, is dislocated, but Randall keeps going, impervious to pain, driven by the love of the collective.

He pants and grunts — throwing himself again and again — and a small crack appears!

The white coated man appears at the doorway.

"Randall!" he screams.

Randall keeps hitting that same small crack.

"Oh shit," the man says, and leaves.

Randall hits that same spot, more times and more frequently than any regular human could. And finally it breaks.

It's not easy. Plexiglass is resilient and will only snap, not shatter. But Randall doesn't care. He pushes against the loose plates until they snap and you are free!

You can sense that in every other cell in the facility, your brethren are breaking free as well.

Suddenly an alarm sounds.

Woah-woah-woah!

Woah-woah-woah!

You and Randall move into the hallway. The white coated man runs toward you, followed by two men in black body armor.

"Oh god, they're out!" the man says.

The men in black pull the white coated man behind them and raise their guns. Gunfire fills the hall and Randall is hit.

"Hit his brain!" the man screams. You trot as fast as you can down the hall and around the men, who are still firing at Randall.

More of your brethren burst from the hall doors and storm the men in black. They raise their guns but are overwhelmed. Randall keeps going.

The white coated woman emerges from a door, sees what's going on, and immediately goes back into her room.

The man runs toward the doors at the end of the hall, pressing a card hung from around his neck to a sensor on the wall. The doors open and the man runs through it. He's not the only one, however. Your brethren move to keep it open. As more of you spill out into the hall, it becomes easier to just follow the white coated man as he opens door after door. Finally you end up in a large room with wide glass doors leading outside.

As the man opens this final set of doors, you lead your brethren toward it.

The doors open like arms.

"They're right behind me!" the man screams into the night.

As you step into the doorway, bright spotlights flare. You hear helicopters in the distance. They shine lights down on you as well.

"Sir!" someone bellows, "Come to us! Come toward the light! We have guns trained on the zombies!"

A chorus of gunfire erupts from below the spotlights. Your brethren are hit!

Randall blinks out. His brain is on the ground behind you.

Panting and slavering, you all march forward, but the guns are too much.

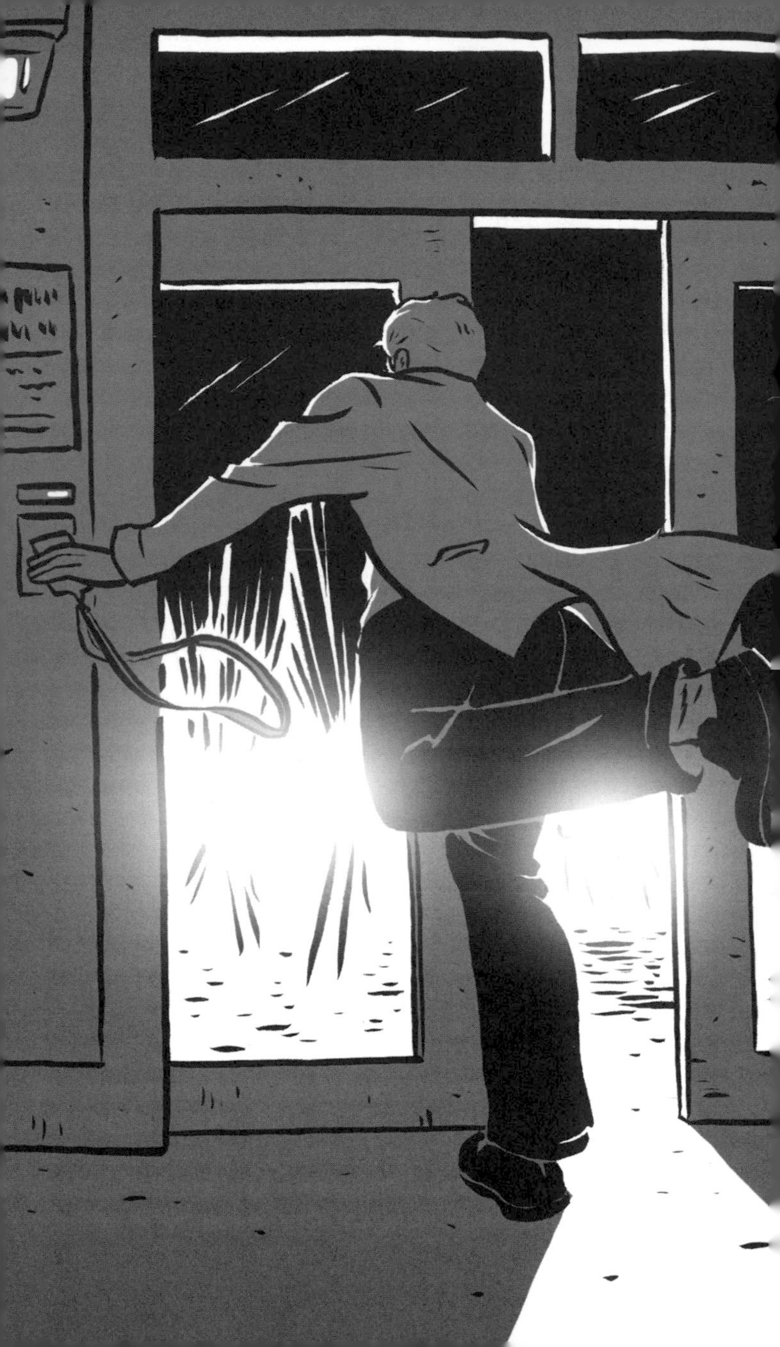

They chip away at your army, taking away your allies one by one, leaving your heart in darkness.

But when you stretch your senses — you feel something else.

"Aaaargh!" the men in front of you scream.

Help has arrived. The community sent an army to help you and here they are.

A spotlight shifts, points down, illuminating the scene for you.

Attacking from behind, your brethren take down the men shooting at you. Their body armor has holes and unprotected joints leaving room for mouths, bites.

You and your stragglers join the feast!

Just like when you were a cat — how you were happiest when everything smelled like you — now everyone and everything will be tainted with your love.

The world's purr rumbles deep inside you, an eternal vibration.

THE END

The next time you open your eyes it's to the sound of a groaning vehicle. Out on the street a battered yellow bus moves slowly. A ragged hole has been cut out of the roof and a man in green sticks out the top holding a long gun. He scans the horizon, regularly bringing the weapon up to his face, then back down.

Cool daylight illuminates the spare parking lot. A number of infected stand idly by, but at the sound of the bus, they lurch to life. More infected seem to spring from the neighbouring lots. As the bus slows to turn into the parking lot, seemingly in seconds a torrent of infected have arrived.

"Mom! Mom!" the older girl shakes her mother awake. "They're here!"

"Fuck, fuck!" the woman mutters to herself, "I was only supposed to sleep for an hour!"

The little girl runs to the front window and leans against the display shelf beside you, looking out. "There's so many zombies!"

The woman makes her way through the aisles and stands behind the both of you.

"Oh god. That's a lot more than last night."

The man with the gun lifts a large megaphone to his mouth.

"This is to anyone inside. Please wait until we have dealt with the infected before emerging. I repeat. Stay inside until we are clear of danger."

Slowly and deliberately, the man starts shooting the infected in their heads. One by one, they drop. Sharp as barks, the gunshots fill the air.

"Oh god, oh god," the woman says under her breath.

Once a number of bodies lie unmoving, the bus inches forward, closer to the store.

But instead of dissipating, the number of infected seems to grow. They come forward and press against the bus, pawing at its windows, pushing against its sides.

The sniper stops to reload, but the infected do not stop. He bends down into the bus and calls to the driver. "There are a lot more of them than I thought. Can you get us closer?"

Other faces stare out the bus windows, horrified.

The sniper resumes his job, but the infected population only grows. More and more close in. The dead bodies start to impede the movement of the bus, getting thick under the wheels.

The woman opens the front door and shouts to the sniper.

"Hey! What if we run to you? Can you hold them off?"

At her presence, the infected closest to the store start in, and press against the gate.

"Ma'am, please stay inside! We'll tell you when it's safe!"

But the infected don't stop. The sheer numbers of them begin to overwhelm the bus. It begins to rock back and forth from their pressure. The people inside start screaming. All through this the sniper is calming dispatching them, but not in enough numbers to make a sizable difference.

Finally he puts his gun away and talks through the megaphone.

"Ma'am! We're not going to be able to retrieve you at this time! We've requested aerial support however! A helicopter is coming! Can you get to the roof?"

"The roof?! Yes, I think we can…"

The bus revs its engines and, bumping over bod-

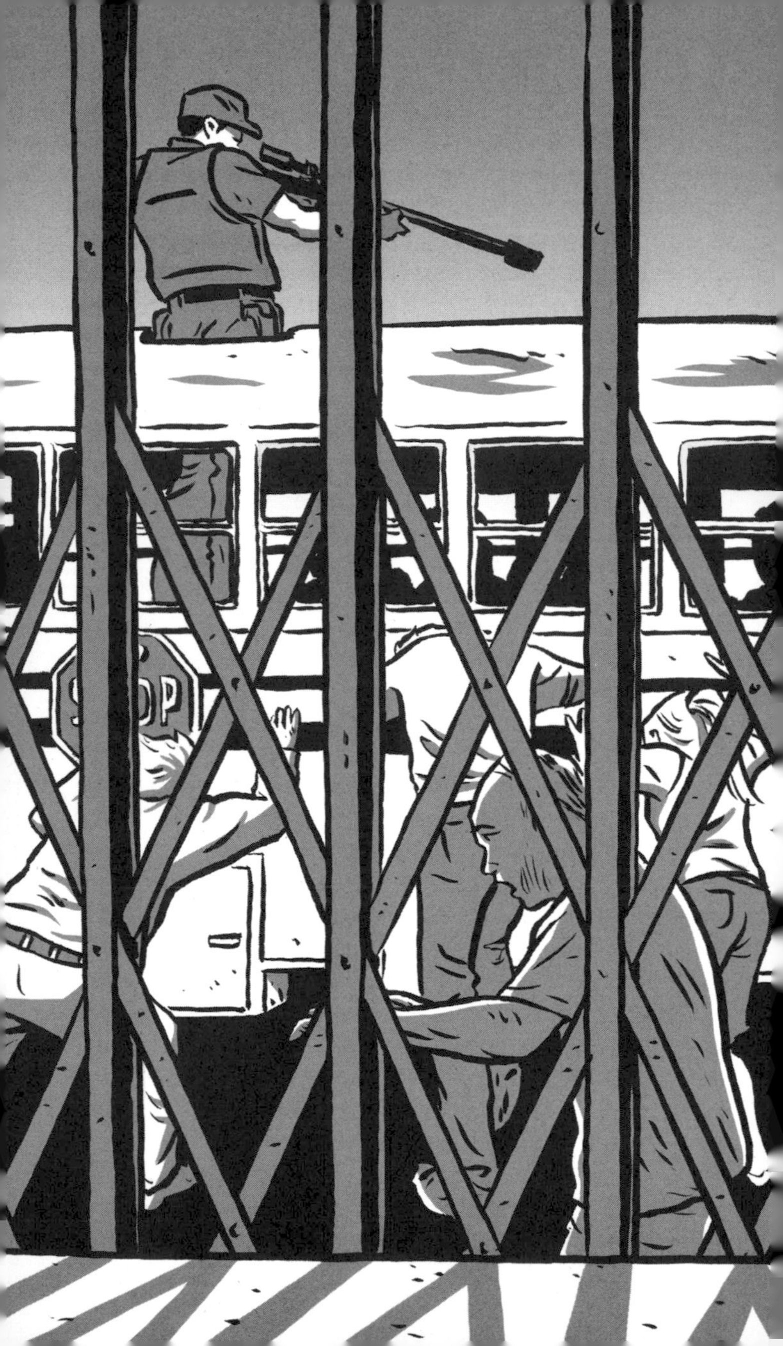

ies, powers its way out to the street. Infected try to stop it, but they are pushed down. Some — run over — still chase it, crawling.

But then a new hunger seems to spread among the infected. The woman closes the door, but the infected continue to bat at the store gate. A growd gathers and they push at it together, seemingly in sync. The woman stares at them, then backs away.

"Girls? C'mon! We're going upstairs."

Almost impossibly, the gate begins to bend.

You get up. Everything's wrong. You run to the back of the store.

The woman gathers the girls up and moves to the door that leads to the basement, but there are stairs going the other way too — upstairs. You decide to follow them.

At the top of the stairs, the woman shoulders a door open and a splash of dawn light spills into the dark stairwell. You jump out onto the roof with them.

Outside it's eerily quiet. You walk over to the edge of the roof and look down. A sea of infected greets you. They are strangely beautiful, the way they pulsate together, pushing at the front gate. They flock, almost like birds in synch.

"There!" the youngest girl points in the air at a small dot.

The *whup-whup-whup* of its rotors drifts toward you.

The woman wanders over to you, peers over the edge.

"Oh god, they almost move like they're co-ordinated or something."

The older girl comes over and places her hands on the edge, also observing.

The rippling bodies retreat, then return. All you can hear is their increased panting, and feel the vibration in the building when they hit it. The infected in the front fall from the force, only to be replaced by more from the back.

The helicopter approaches. You have seen many of them in the sky before, but never this close. You are surprised by how loud they are. The downblast of air flattens your ears for you.

And amid all the noise, you hear a huge boom, and suddenly the infected surge into the doorway, breaking the inside glass door, and enter the building.

"Oh god! Mom!' the older girl screams. "They're inside."

A stricken look flits across the woman's face. Then she runs back to the door.

"Help me!" she says to her daughters. "Help me hold it closed!"

The three humans press their backs against the door and close their eyes in terrible anticipation.

All the while the helicopter gets larger and larger, and the sky gets lighter and lighter. It is fiercely windy on the roof. Windier than you have ever experienced. The woman is shouting at her kids, but whatever she's saying is lost.

Finally the helicopter is at the roof. It's a large roof, that extends the length of all the stores, but various structures on it deter landing. Instead, it hooks its landing strut over the roof edge while the rest of it hovers. Its door slides opens and a man in a blue shirt beckons the family.

The woman pushes her children forward.

They look back at her and say something, but the sound of the rotors fills the air entirely.

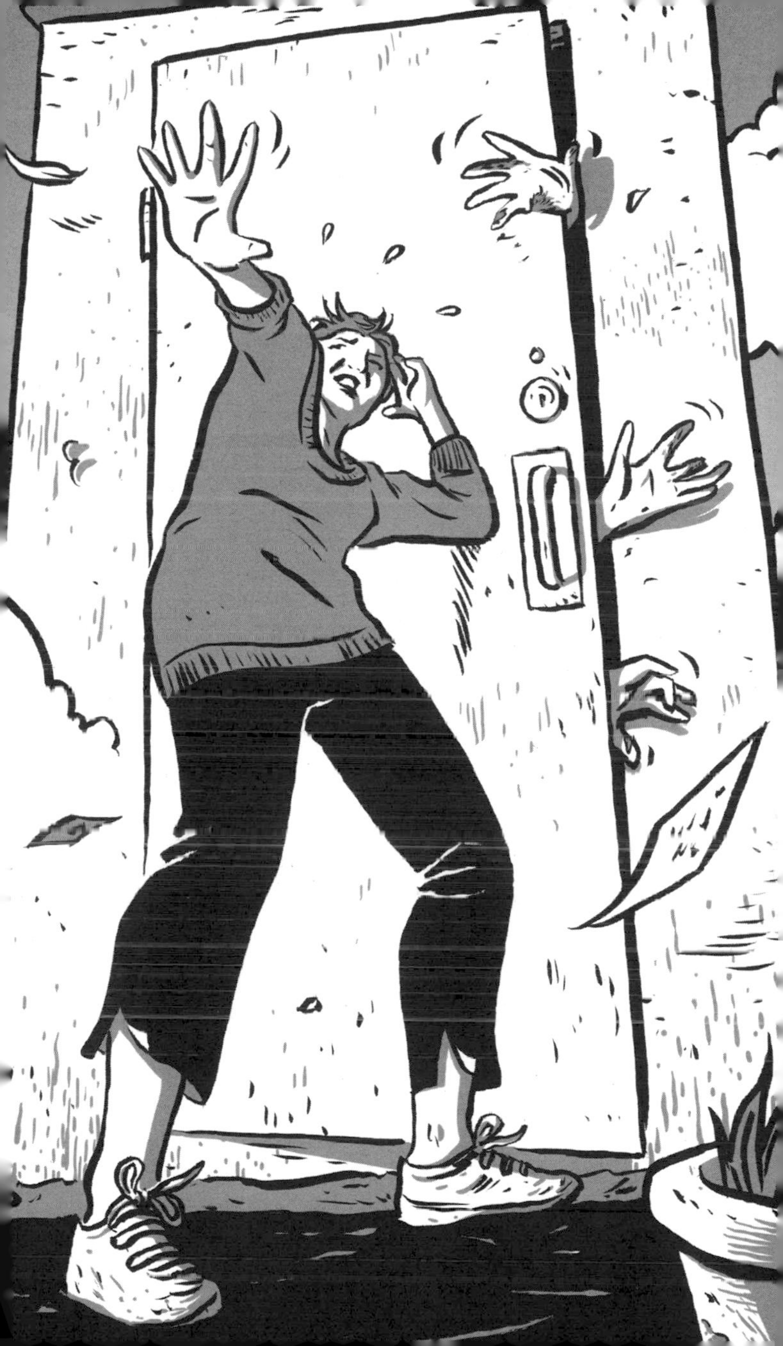

"Go!" the woman screams, but it is just her mouth open in an O.

The girls run toward the helicopter.

Behind the woman, the door bucks open for a moment, but the woman pushes it closed.

It bucks again.

Rabid hands claw out!

At the helicopter, the man in the blue shirt helps the girls on board, then looks at the woman, beckoning. Finally the woman lets go of the door and runs.

As she races forward, the infected burst out through the door.

Uh oh.

If you jump to another rooftop turn to page 50.

If you run after the woman, turn to page 237.

Over the years you've discovered that sometimes the best thing you can do is nothing. In fact, you do nothing a lot. Sometimes you hang out, just observing. This is what you do today. You sit and gaze down to the end of the alley.

And sure enough — something happens. A small truck comes down toward you.

When it gets too close for comfort, however, you dart behind a trash can and underneath a fence out of sight.

The truck slows and stops. You hear someone get out.

"I saw him," a woman says. She sounds odd. Her nose is stuffed up, like she's sick. "He ducked behind this bin... Kitty! Here kitty..."

You peek underneath the fence and see some shoes. A woman in a white coat and blue rubber gloves is crouched and looking for you. When she sees you, she smiles. She reaches into her pocket and pulls out a small container. Something rattles inside it.

It sounds like a treat!

The woman pulls the lid off the container and pulls out a nugget of something. It reeks of fish and meat and something else besides. The aroma radiates off of it like heat.

"He's over here! I found him!" the woman calls out.

You hear someone else get out of the truck.

You're wary, but it's hard to leave. The scent of the nugget has you transfixed.

"Collar?" the man behind the woman says.

"Can't see any."

The woman drops the nugget on the ground in front of you!

Immediately you descend on it. It smells so good you can just about taste it in the air before it hits your tongue.

"Feral?"

"Don't know," the woman says. "He seems a little well-fed to be feral."

"You know the policy."

The woman nods. As you are eating the nugget, she lifts you up in one swift movement and tosses you in a cat carrier the man holds open! Quickly, they shut the wire door and lock it.

Shocked, you don't do anything for a moment. The man walks you behind the truck and opens the back door. Inside, you see more carriers on shelves built into the walls. You hear meowls of complaint coming from other cats.

This was a terrible mistake. You shouldn't have trusted that woman. But she tricked you with her treats. Now you meowl too.

The man slides you into a spot on the shelf, then draws a kind of netting in front of your cage, clicking something into place. Then he leaves, and shuts the door. Now the only lighting comes in from the front window.

The man slides into a seat in front.

"Hey," the woman says, "I just got a text from Alice. They want us to come back."

"What's up?"

"Not sure. Some kind of incident. Reports of some animals behaving oddly. Anyway, they might need the truck."

"All right."

For the next while you complain loudly. You lend your caterwauling to the chorus of other cats but the humans in front don't seem to notice. From across the van, you smell another cat's piss. It's either upset, or it couldn't hold it any longer.

Finally the van eases to a stop.

The woman glances at her phone.

"Perfect timing," she says. "Just in time for my coffee break."

"Where are you going? Across the street?"

"Not sure. Want something?"

"I might come with. I didn't have breakfast."

The humans leave, and you're left with the sound of one cat who, every few seconds, meows out a complaint.

You close your eyes and try to imagine you are somewhere else but the meows you hear keep dragging you back to reality. You are usually very good at drowning out noise while you sleep, but this situation is too stressful for you to fully relax.

Eventually you nod off and your damned neighbour shuts up.

When you wake up, you examine the light inside the van. You try to gauge how much time has passed.

A lot.

You really have to take a shit, but you don't want to do it here. There's no litter. It would feel weird. And then you would have to sit beside it as it reeks.

Over time, the light dims, and then it's dark.

Other cats in the van don't have your self-control, and soon the smell of other cats' piss and shit fill the van. It's overwhelming. The chorus of complaints start again.

This is awful.

What are the humans doing? Why are they doing this to me?

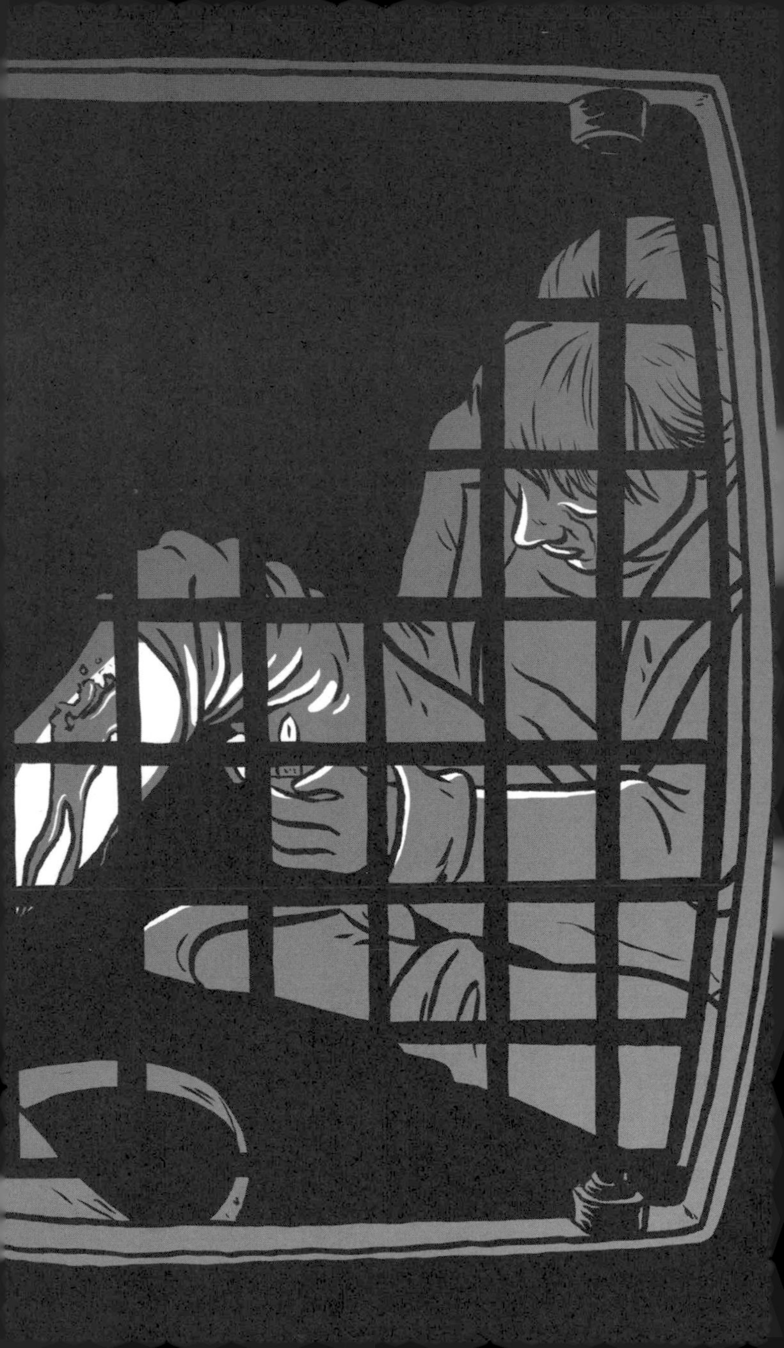

Finally, a noise.

The backdoor creaks open and the woman with the cold slides in. She closes the door behind her and lies on the floor of the van in darkness.

A different smell mingles with the awful cocktail of cat excrement — the woman's fear.

She shakes as she lets out sob after sob. Most of the cats quieten, except for that one who keeps meowing.

When the woman has finished sobbing, she reaches into her purse and pulls something out. It's too dark to see. You hear a high metallic clink, then a sharp rasp and then — a spark appears!

Then another spark!

"Fucking Zippo," the woman mutters. "Light already."

Suddenly a flame appears in the woman's hand.

You stare at her. Her white coat is dotted with blood. She moves the flame and examines her leg. It's bleeding on her calf.

"Oh fuck, I'm screwed. I'm screwed!"

The flame is placed on the floor and you watch the woman reach into her purse. She pulls out a bunch of items which you recognize from the vet.

You hate the vet.

That place always smells awful.

You shrink back in your cage.

You meow at the woman. You hate this.

She looks up at you, then goes back to what she was doing.

"There's a better world somewhere, kitty."

Eventually she shrugs off her white coat and rolls up her sleeve. She ties a rope around her arm and brings the flame up to it. She examines her skin a moment and then puts the flame down. She lifts a needle up to her arm, inserts it and squeezes it.

"Sure ain't this one."

She lets out a little noise, then drops the needle, unties the rope, and the flame disappears.

Then the woman falls alseep.

Or at least you think she falls aslseep, but moments later, her body convulses on the floor!

The thumping lasts for a bit, then stops. She chokes, lets out a ragged breath, then doesn't move.

It is quiet for a long time, then —

"Heh, heh," the woman says. "Heh."

Slowly, she wrenches her body to its knees and comes to your cage. You move to the very back of it, trying to stay away from her fingers and her wretched scent. She is relentless in her pursuit of you, but unable somehow to work the mechanism to open the cage. Later she will go after some of the other cats in their cages, but have similar difficulties.

Eventually, after a few days, you are so thirsty, you can't even think.

Blessedly, you black out.

Blessedly, you never regain consciousness.

THE END

The woman races to the helicopter and the man in blue helps her onboard. She hugs her little ones when she's inside.

Then the youngest girl sees you and shouts, "Wait, wait!" at the man, pointing excitedly. She leans dangerously out, arms open.

You gallop, tearing along the rooftop, finally leaping from the edge!

Time seems to slow down. You see the girl's excited eyes. The man in blue's furrowed brow. The girls' arms are out like a lap, waiting to hold you. You have never been more sure of anything in your life — that if you reach them, she will grasp you, and pull you inside, and you will be safe.

A moment in mid-air —

The girl grabs you, bringing you to her chest!

"Whoa, whoa!" the man yells. It's very loud in the helicopter. You can hardly hear him. He reaches over to you and tries to forcefully pry you from the girl's arms.

Suddenly, the helicopter dips!

The man peers over the edge and sees a few of the infected hooking onto the landing strut with their arms. They look up with frenzied eyes.

The man grabs a small axe from the wall and leans out the door. He starts by kicking at them, but when that doesn't work he chops at their arms. Meanwhile the helicopter swings sickeningly in circles as it tries to ditch the excess weight.

Finally the man leans back inside. He doesn't have the axe anymore, and the helicopter rises up into the air.

He takes you from the little girl and examines you. When he's satisfied, he returns you to her and

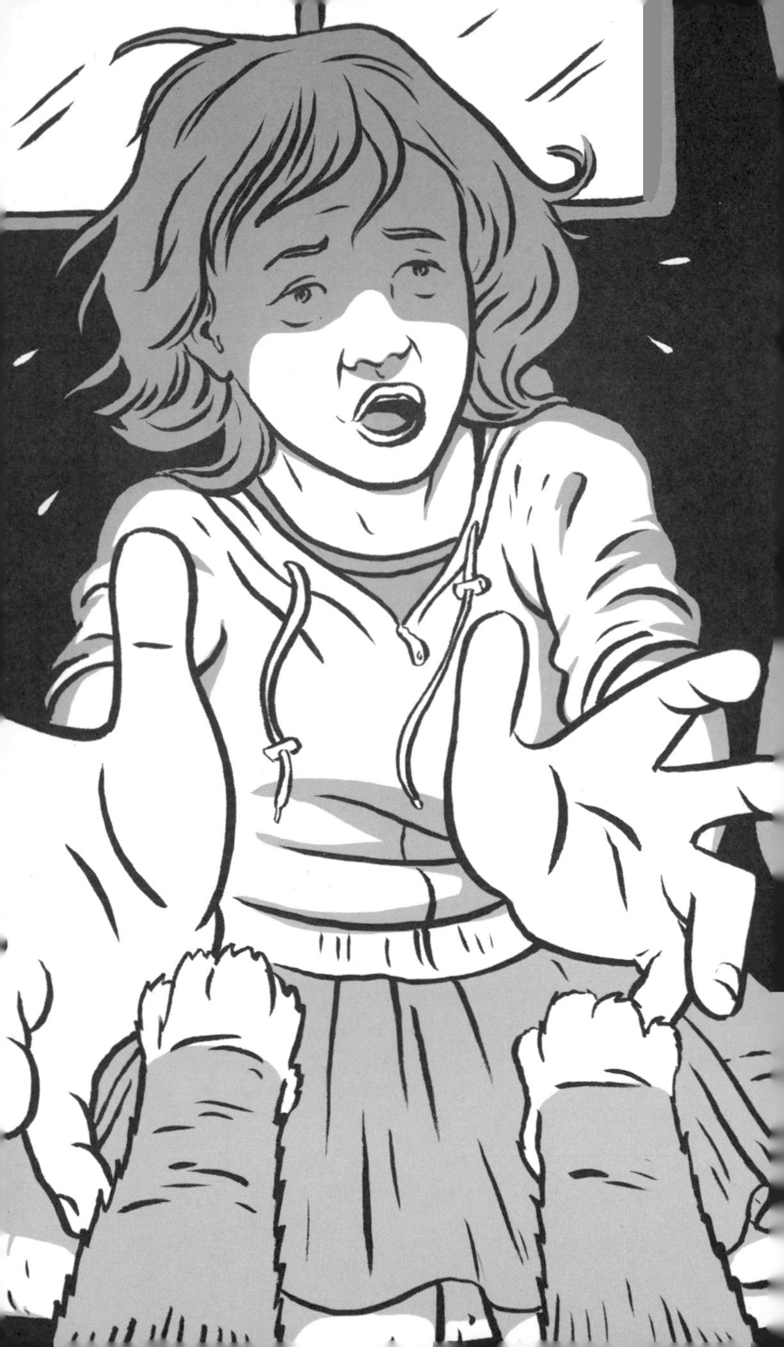

leans back, exhausted in his seat.

Looking out the window, you see the bus from earlier, on its side, overrun.

Somewhere down there is your girlfriend.

In the years to come, after temporary residencies in various camps, and then a relocation to a small farm, you'll stay with this family. They will rename you Lucky. Sometimes they will call you Lucky Charms. And sometimes Mr. Charms. Or Mr. Charming.

You'll be with them as these two young girls become young women.

You will live a long and comfortable life.

And then one day you will die safe and warm and you will be with your girlfriend again.

THE END

The car coughs.

It sluggishly starts, then rouses itself into motion.

The headlights come on, illuminating the woods. The girl holds you to her chest, less to comfort you than to comfort herself.

"Hold on," the stranger says, a waver in her voice. "I gotta 3-point turn."

"What?!" the girl turns to her.

"Got to. It's narrow here. We could end up in a ditch."

A distant scream from inside the cabin.

"Oh god," the girl says, putting her face into your fur, "they're eating him."

As the car goes through its delicate maneuvers, the headlights spotlight something.

"What is that?!" the girl screams.

The girls stare. The scene is surreal. Emerging from the woods is a gigantic beast. The size of a small car itself, its fur matted and wet, its eyes red.

"Fuck," the stranger says, "Bear."

"Bear?!"

The beast shambles out — surprisingly fast for something so big — toward the car.

The wheels spin, flicking gravel behind you.

"Go go!"

The beast rears up in front. This close, you can see its foaming mouth, its slick nose, its bloody eyes. One of its lips has already started peeling away, exposing black gums and yellowing teeth.

The stranger tries to steer around, but the bear is too big. The car front clips the bear's leg with a thud. Its falls into the side of the car, spiderwebbing a side window.

"Keep going!" the girl urges.

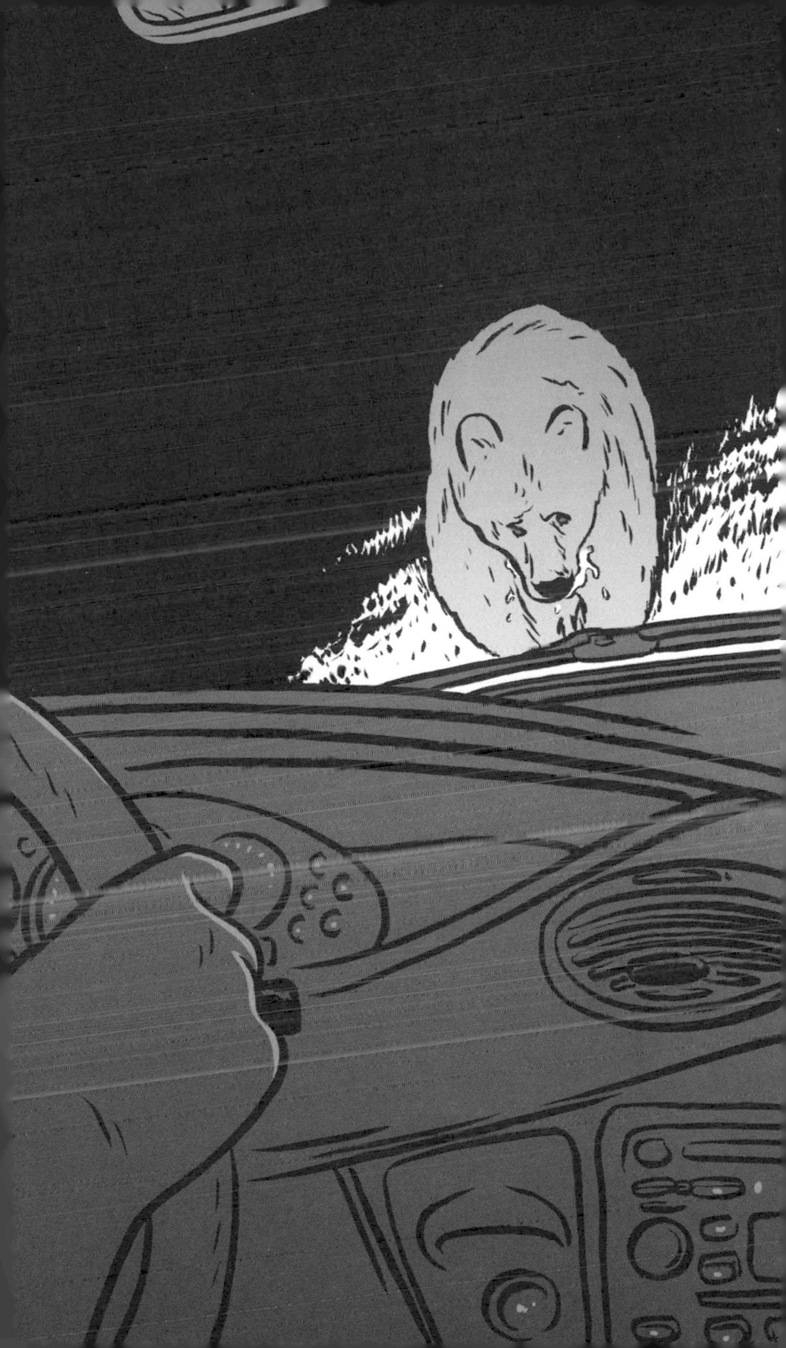

"I'm not stopping."

With a sudden burst of speed, the car pulls away from the bear. A thud from behind as the bear swipes at it. But soon you've outpaced the beast and are back on the paved highway.

"Where are we going?" the girl asks. She's finally stopped clutching you so tightly.

The stranger doesn't answer. She's breathing hard. In the darkness you can see her forearms trembling.

"Amanda?" the girl turns. "You okay?"

The stranger is silent for a second. Then when she speaks, her voice comes out in a warble, barely keeping its emotions in check.

"I don't know," the stranger says. "Our cabin's overrun. It's not safe anymore. I don't know where my parents are. They should have been here by now. We should have — " The stranger's voice is trembling. The girl puts her arm around her.

"Amanda, it's okay."

The stranger pulls the car over, starts crying. The car rumbles to a halt underneath you.

"I don't know. I don't know where to go. We've got a quarter tank left. My parents are probably dead. There's no food. We're going to die. We're going to fucking *die!*"

The girl nods.

"I know," she says soothingly.

"It's the end of everything," the stranger says, "I mean, what in the hell? What the fuck? I was just beginning to get my life together. I mean — start dating you, paying off this thing — " The stranger slams a palm into the steering wheel.

"I know," the girl says. Now she's weeping too.

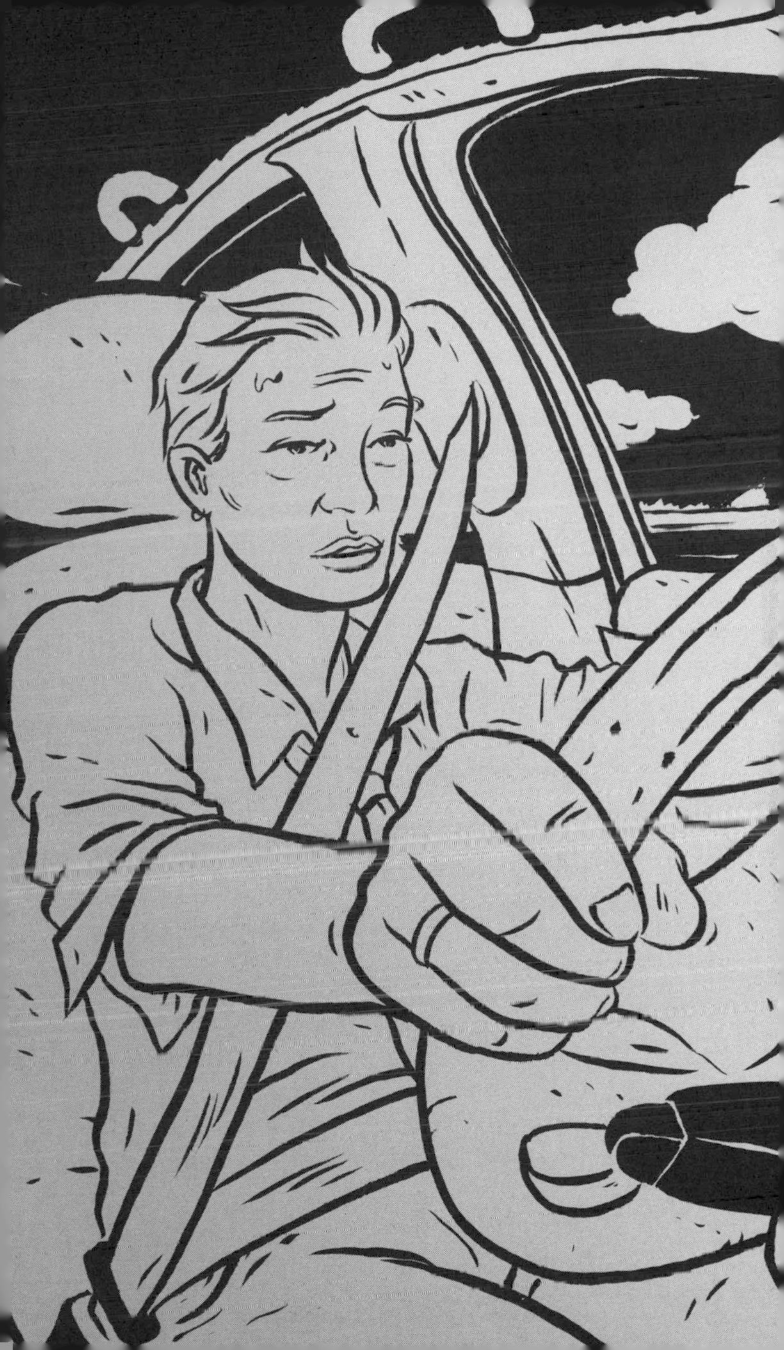

Wet tears drop onto your fur. Annoyed, you get up. You jump up onto the dash, your back feet finding purchase on the knobs and buttons on the centre console.

A buzz.

"What's that?" the girl asks.

"Your cat turned on the radio."

"— gain, this is the Armed Forces, we have set up refugee camps for anyone who can understand this, at the following locations: Pickering. Bowmanville. Cobourg..."

"Oh my god!"

The girls talk excitedly among themselves some more. You press your head into the cool glass and look at them. Their mood's changed. You don't know why, but they are happier now.

The car starts up, and the dash rumbles to life.

The girl turns on the overhead light and opens a book. She puts her finger on a dot that's nested in a web of interconnected lines.

"Bowmanville. That's closest."

The stranger laughs.

"Maybe we can make it."

You clamber down off the dash and onto the girl's lap. You like that they are happier. You fall asleep.

It's a long drive but you are grateful for this long period of inaction and calm. You've had enough excitement to last a good long while.

You don't wake until a rosy pink light fills the sky outside the window. You look up at the girl, who is asleep in her chair. You yawn and stretch.

The stranger looks over at you.

"Hey Holden," she says. "Good morning."

The girl rouses awake and opens her sleepy eyes.

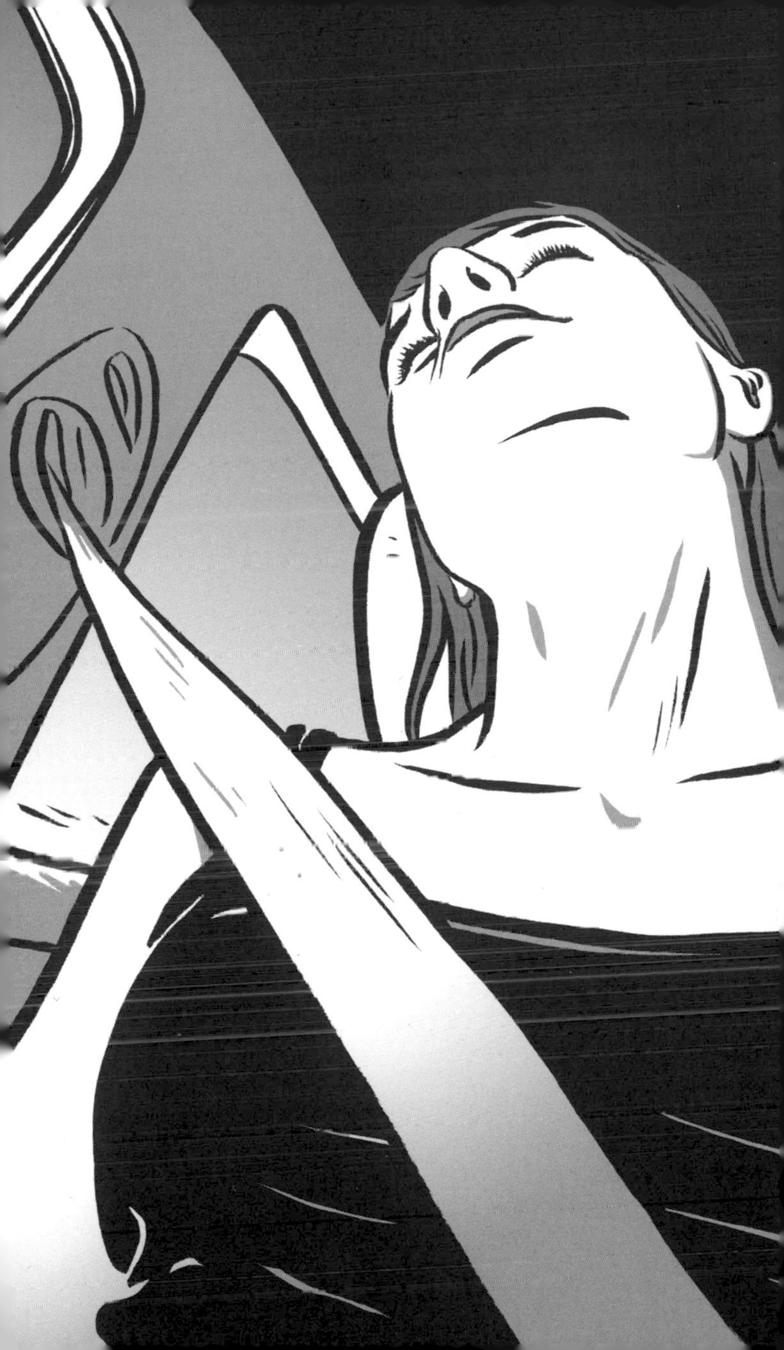

She looks out the window and her eyes widen.

"Holy shit. Is that it?" the girl asks.

"Tents and trucks? Yeah, I guess that's it."

The girl leans forward. What is she looking at?

You jump up onto the dash and look out.

A buzz of activity inside a fenced-in compound. People mill among uncountable numbers of tents. Large green trucks and vehicles line up inside and outside the camp. Men and women in green stand sentry with large mounted guns.

You turn to look at the girls, their faces tear-streaked, open with expectation. The car stops.

"You in the car!" A man's voice, unusually loud, echoes through the window. "Drive slowly into the receiving area when we open the gates! When you're inside, shut the engine completely off! Wave if you understand!"

The girls wave their arms. The car moves again, slowly.

You watch as the stranger's hand finds the girl's.

Your stomach rumbles.

You don't know what's going on, but you have this feeling you are going to eat soon, and that is a really good feeling.

For the first time in what seems like forever you purr.

THE END

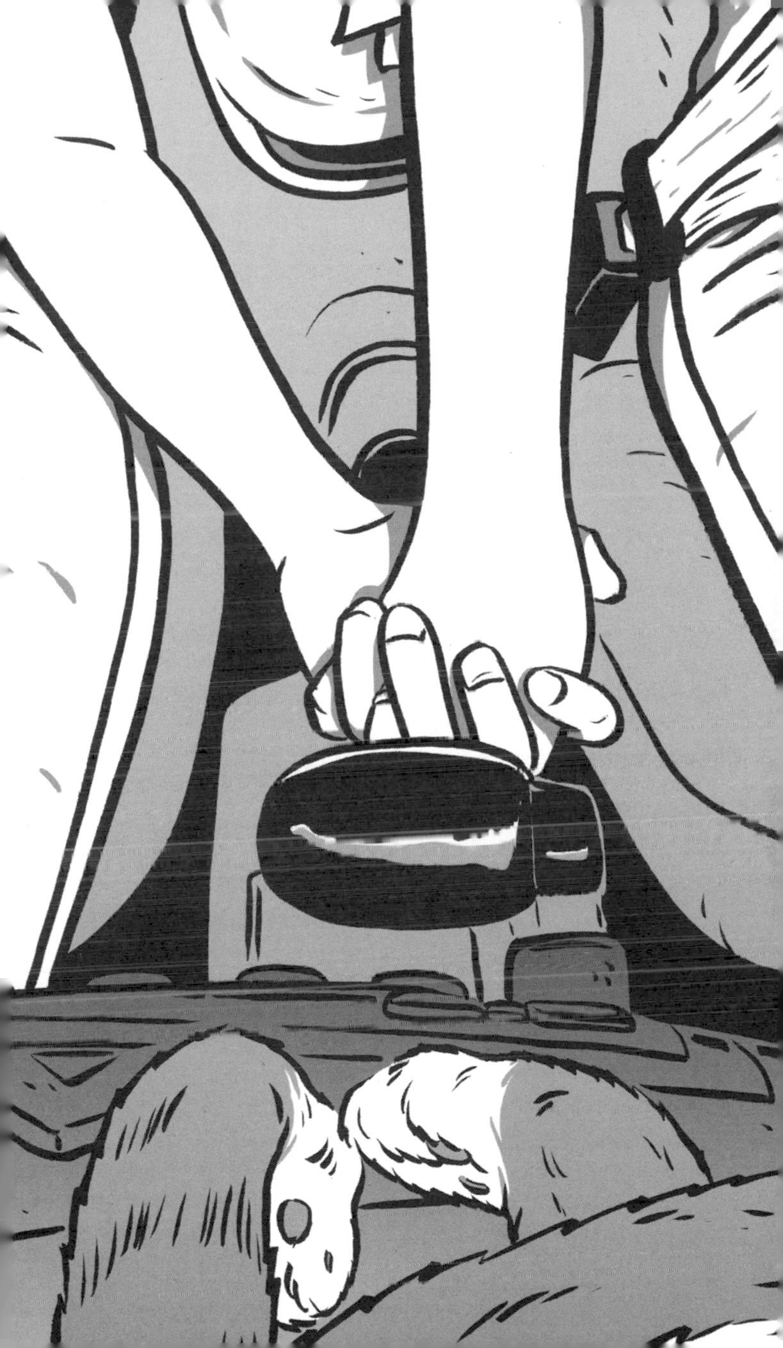

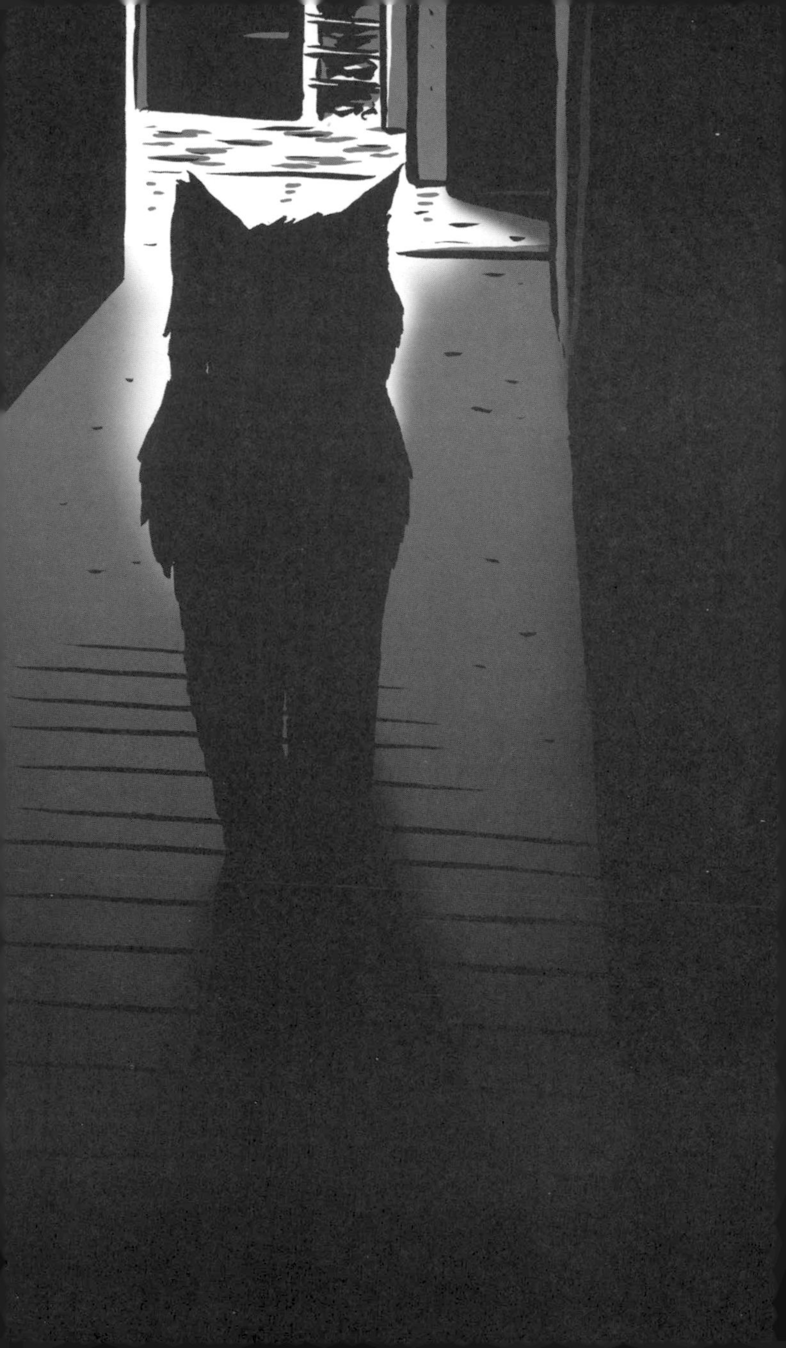

Catknowledgements

Frankly, the premise sounded like a joke. *A Choose-Your-Own-Adventure style book from the POV of a housecat? What are your choices? To nap or to eat?* Well, yes. But the book presumed more than that. It presupposed that the life of a cat is a lot more interesting and exciting than you would think, and that once it gets outside — well, an amazing adventure awaits.

Two years ago, when the first book in this series came out, I wasn't thinking sequel. *You Are a Cat!* was pretty preposterous. I was simply delighted to be getting away with making such an outlandish thing in the first place. But what I remembered the most about its creation was what an absolute blast I had, from conception, to sketching out the paths and choices, to getting into the mind of Holden Catfield — his particular blend of curiosity and directness — and then the charm of getting to create illustrations from his first-purrson POV.

So it was easy for me to revisit that world with *You Are a Cat in the Zombie Apocalypse!*. If I'm being perfectly honest, I was a *little* worried about the zombie aspect. I thought that maybe zombies were played out. And they might be. But then, they said the same thing about vampires and giant robots and superheroes. Maybe these interests aren't flashy fads but rather the natural growth of an entire genre. So when my publisher gave the sequel a greenlight I went full-bore. What *would* it be like to be a cat during a zombie apocalypse? You hold the result in your perfect little paws!

I just hope my publisher will also greenlight the *prequel* I want to make, to turn this two book series into a trilogy with *You Are a Kitten!* Holden's formative years: first falls, first loves, first hacking up of hairballs. The story of how he got his charming name, and finally found his forever home. Or *will* he find it? It's up to you! You make the choices! You pick the plot!

So thank you. Thank you to those who bought the first book and thanks to those who purchased this improbable sequel. Thank you for taking a chance on weird, ridiculous books. Your support makes it easier for even *weirder* things to get made. And I really appreciate that because those quirky things are all I am drawn to create.

I want to thank my family — my brother Sean, his girlfriend Steph, my mom and my dad and my extended family for their support and love over the years and into the future.

I want to thank the following people, who, in very particular ways, contributed to the creation of this very particular book: Al L, Amber G, Amy B, Amy D, Andrea JR, Bess WK, Billy M, Catherine P, Dawn K, Elena T, Emilie O'B, Farshid E, Glenna G, Ian SC, Ian F, Indigo E, Jenny L, Joe O, Jo W, Joey D, Julia B, Kimura B, Louis R, Luna A, Lynn C, Margaux W, Megan H, Miriam G, Robin H, Ryan K, Shie K, Sofi P, Stephen WW, Tori A, and Vince T.

Thanks to Orion and Altaire and Roy and Jo, who, with their warm house full of animals, first lit for me my lifelong love for cats.

Thanks to Alex G, Anthony H, Courtney W, Bernie M, for kindly and without reservation posing for the pictures which helped me work out numerous purrspective problems in the first-purrson pictures that finally appear here. Thanks to Eliane E for the use of her car! Thanks to Laurie P and Seymour! Thanks to Janelle H and Chat! Thanks to Kimura B and Pangu! I am grateful for your help!

Thanks to the cats who have taught me everything I know about verve, daring, calmness and patience: Kara and Cohen. Joe. Sully. JJ. Miccio and Gigi. Rosa. Ali, Rosa, Dirty, Gina and Gloria. Pinky. Rosie. Khan. Mia. Morris. Coco. Jingxi and Margaux. Blanche and Sophie. The late October.

Thanks to my Facebook "friends". I understand that a Facebook relationship is tenuous and complicated, and while some people find Facebook invasive and superficial, I have found it nothing but a scintillating revelation, and am proud to engage in this global village conversation every day with all of you. Anyone reading this who isn't already my friend should like, totally friend me.

Thanks to Andy B at Conundrum Towers for taking a chance on this madness. I keep making weird things, and you keep saying, "Let me have a look." You and your curiousity coaxed this cat out of me, and I thank you.

Thanks to Elena T for your friendship, your bravery, your appetite for experience, and continued wonderfulness.

Thanks to Kailey B, for all the things.